My lads showing an example of caff sand.
(Kevin Alexander collection).

Front cover; Jim Alexander snr aboard his boat Susan.

TALES OF THE DUDDON SANDS

TALES OF THE DUDDON SANDS

a compilation of forgotten maritime stories

KEVIN ALEXANDER

KEVIN ALEXANDER

Copyright © 2023 by Kevin Alexander

All rights reserved. No part of this book may be reproduced in any manner whatsoever without written permission except in the case of brief quotations embodied in critical articles and reviews.

First Printing, 2024, by www.ingramspark.com.

Proofread by Racheal Bloom, Mary Borgia and Kelly Alexander.

A catalogue record for this book is available from the British Library.

ISBN 978-1-3999-7566-7

CONTENTS

Photo Insert		i
INTRODUCTION		ix
One	MY FAMILY, THE ALEXANDER'S	1
Two	GLOSSARY	6
Three	A LIST OF SHIPWRECKS	8
Four	SHIPWRECKS AND TRAGEDIES	9
Five	RESCUES AND NEAR MISSES	34
Six	IN TROUBLE WITH THE LAW	38
Seven	OTHER BITS AND BOBS	58
Photo Insert		71
ACKNOWLEDGEMENTS		73

INTRODUCTION

The beautiful Duddon Sands, a quiet and tranquil place. Not much goes on here nowadays other than folk walking dogs or the odd recreational fisherman catching a fish or two. However, this wasn't always the case; the Duddon once hosted two large centres of industry one on either side of the estuary. Millom in Cumberland and Askam in Lancashire. Both had iron mines and ironworks close to the sands creating noise and action, increasing both shipping and population. The latter would go to the shore for recreation. Crowds of holiday makers would travel from afar to spend the day on the shores at Askam, Haverigg or Sandscale.

School children bathing at Askam Shore.
(Kevin Alexander collection).

The sands also held a healthy fishery, with a small community of fisherfolk covering the sands at low water to gather mussels and cockles and fish from stake nets, and then out again at hightide in their boats. All this busy activity has now gone, almost unbelievable today as you stand and look out across the vast and empty estuary.

I have only known the sands in this quiet state as all the industry had long gone before I was born. My early years were spent playing on the shore with my mates, making dens in the dunes or messing about down Askam Pier catching crabs and babby flukes in the gutters and sitting in my grandad's boat while the tide came in, pretending I were a pirate and the like. We would go bait digging for lug or rag worm and then go rodding off the pier or string a longline out and see what we got, then fetch home the catch for our parents to sort out.

Come wintertime and the bad weather, I remember our dad would take me onto the shore to watch the white horse waves crashing onto the dunes and then walk out along the pier, almost sidewards fighting the wind as we watched the waves come flying right over to the other side. This is still an activity I enjoy doing; you cannot beat free entertainment!

Naturally over the years I have picked up an interest in the history of where I live and from where I come from, and whenever I came across anything relating to the Duddon, I would jot it down and forget about it. It has got to the point where no book exists about the Duddon Sands alone and next to nothing is mentioned about the maritime fishing folk or ordinary folk that once occupied the sands, so here we are, I suppose I might as well put this attempt forward myself and hope the reader finds the following as interesting as I have found it to be, and maybe next time on the sands some of these stories come to mind.

The industrial past I may add, has been recognised, and that has been written about in great detail and brilliantly in the following books; *Millom, a Cumberland iron town and its railways, by Alan Atkinson,* and also in *Northwestern ships and seamen, by Alan Lockett.* Both books are worth obtaining if you are truly interested in the Duddon Estuary. The detail to Millom's shipbuilding and sailing history in the latter book is worthy of being a book in its own right, I had permission from Alan Lockett's family to reproduce the Millom section of that book here, but I have reluctantly refrained from doing so. Instead, I would like to portray the history and stories of the folk that ventured onto the sands and estuary from the 19th and early 20th century, mainly that of the old fisherfolk using reports and newspaper articles from that time, giving an insight into those forgotten maritime families of the Duddon, including my own.

| one |

MY FAMILY, THE ALEXANDER'S

Teddy Alexander in the old pen.
(Walter Jinks collection).

I grew up in a typical terrace house up on the Lots in Askam, literally feet away from the shore in the very same house my great grandparents, Jim and Nellie Alexander had lived. Right at the top of the shore and near to the house was what I knew as the old Alexander pen. A fenced in allotment/small holding, with fisherman's huts made from driftwood and salvaged rusty corrugated tins that probably came from the mines or ironworks. It looked at that time derelict and almost abandoned, with a thick covering of brambles and nettles. It was full of ancient artifacts to me. I remember it had an old Ford T truck and old engines and loads and loads of old boating and fishing gear, an absolute Aladdin's cave to me, which I wish I could go back to now! However unfortunately it has long gone and now mostly reverted back to nature apart from some iron fencing and timber fence posts.

We had our very own Alexander pen by the old iron ore mine, in fact I still have it, and again it used to be my great grandparents. My grandad made it after the Second World War to store his fishing gear in and he also kept pigs and poultry and grew vegetables. His older brother, Teddy, had taken over their dad's one at the top of the shore as he wanted his own spot; in fact, there were once eight family pens on the Lots, mainly dedicated to the pursuit of fishing.

Just down the road from my house lived an old lass, my great grandad's sister, old aunt Jane Brown with her old Bakelite glasses. She was a small lady, but still, she was a formidable person. She would call me over shouting "laal barn," (*small child*) and we would have random chats about school and the like, she even taught me how to peg the washing out for it not to disappear in the

Possibly John Jinks Snr on horse and Jim Alexander Jr in the old pen.
(Walter Jinks collection).

wild westerly winds that we get on the Lots, and yes there is a correct way of doing it where even in a gale it'll be on the line still.

She spoke with the old dialect of Furness that I imagine the rest of our family once spoke. It is, on the whole, hardly in use anymore in the district and also now very watered down, just a few words are spoken here and there. I thank her and my great grandad Doug Moore, whose family hailed from Hallthwaites, for my knowledge of it, as without them speaking it and passing it on within the family these words would more than likely disappear from use. I have compiled a small glossary of mainly shore related words in the coming pages.

Further down the street from Jane were more Alexander relatives, more on the next street over and again the street behind me. Distant relatives seemed to be all over the spot, and I would see them day to day throughout the years, and it's with talking to them about the family that I have gained good knowledge of our past and about the shore. Distant cousins Walter and John Jinks (both fished the Duddon all their lives) and my great Aunt Muriel Wilson have contributed the most, for which I'm forever grateful.

The Alexander's, originally being stone masons and quarrymen, came to Askam then known as Ireleth Marsh, from a village called Over Kellet near Lancaster, to work in the iron mines in 1870. The spot was a building site with it's creation only beginning five years earlier, with no sewers, no paved streets not even any trees. It was a barren, sandy, windswept place as there was no pier or slagbank offering shelter. They only started later on with the pier in 1898 partly as a way of sheltering the settlement and a way of getting rid of the waste slag, they extending it several times until it was abandoned in 1918.

It was normal that the sand would bank up against the houses, creating sand dunes in the street as high as the bedroom windows, with folk having to dig themselves out! Even to this day when it's windy we get sand all over the cars and windows of the houses, but nothing like they got mind.

Three sons followed their father into the Askam mines, although all three left the village in 1889 to search for greater opportunities due to an iron recession at the time.

William - my great, great grandad and Thomas went to the Kimberly diamond mine in South Africa, and Edward went to a coal mine in Walkden, Manchester. Sadly Thomas died while on a train journey outside of Cape Town, so my great, great grandad William Alexander, came back to Askam in 1890 where he married Rebecca Gilchrist.

They moved to Walkden, to join the other brother Edward, where they settled and had a couple of children. During this time in Manchester, family lore has it that William either damaged his leg badly or lost it completely resulting in him being unable to mine anymore and so back to Askam they went. Rebecca's older brothers were Proctor's that already fished the Duddon, and so William and Rebecca took to the trade as well. (This would be around 1894).

William bought a Mussel boat from Overton, near Lancaster, called the Lunesdale, which was the name of the valley our family had originally come from.

It was a hard life and existence being a fishing family at that time, however they prospered, having eleven children. (Hence the abundance of relatives today). All of them (apart from John, who died due to accidentally burning himself on the kitchen fire aged six), went on to fish, even the lasses too. They gathered Mussels with a large rake at Sandscale, using horse and cart to fetch off, or if further out the boat was used. Cockles were gathered with a rake and cram, and again the horse would have been used. But by the 1950's, my grandad was using grey Ferguson tractors instead and another relative used Fordsons. They kept a stake net off Lots Shore that was in and around the same spot for over 70 years, known as the "Alexander stakes". The whole family tended to the net, mainly catching flukes and plaice. A drawnet was also used from the boat to catch Salmon and they used a beam trawl for shrimps and flat fish.

The boat, Lunesdale, was originally used under oar. Later a small petrol engine was added. They would take it off the boat every day during the winter and keep it warm in the oven at home so it would fire up ok for them the next day, as it was a devil to get going again without.

Jim Alexander snr (standing), Jim Alexander jr (toddler) and Billy Jinks (lad) on the family horse used for fishing before tractors. Victoria Street Askam.
(Kevin Alexander collection).

William Alexander, Unknown Bird, Unknown Tyson.
(Walter Jinks collection).

Unknown Bird, William Alexander, Unknown Tyson, aboard Lunesdale, circa 1900, with a drawnet for Salmon fishing.
(Walter Jinks collection).

My great grandad, Jim, ended up with the boat and his son, my grandad Jim junior, fibre glassed the hull in the 1970's after it had hit Askam Pier. I can remember it painted red outside our pen in around 1996, before my grandad cut it up. I've still got the keel band, and bits of the keel, and two of the three original oars to this day. My dad remembers going out on it as a lad in the middle of the night with my grandad and great grandad. The latter would scull while my dad and grandad would shoot the net in the hope of catching a few silver fellas.

Jim Alexander snr at his Pen.
(Kevin Alexander collection).

Our other boat was called Susan, registration BW138. Great grandad found it washed up on Lots Shore in the 1930's. It was an Irish clinker built lifeboat that had been blown off a ferry in a storm. The ferry company told him to keep it as it was cheaper to have one made than recover it. He sold it to a butcher from Barrow in 1939 before he went in the Navy during the Second World War so granny would have some money while he was away. Thankfully, he survived the war and the boat survived in Walney Channel despite the bombing of Barrow and he was able to buy it back. He first set it up for sailing and later he put in an air-cooled Enfield twin cylinder engine, the boat just about survives as a wreck today beside Askam Pier and you can still see the port registration on its sides.

My great grandad Jim, like his brothers, became a part-time fisherman as there was better, more reliable money to be had elsewhere. He got a job on the cranes in the shipyard at Barrow and my grandad, Jim Junior, joined him serving his apprenticeship in the yard. He then left for the merchant navy in New Zealand before eventually coming back home and back into the shipyard again, ending up as a diesel engineer, overseeing quality control as an inspector.

They both sold their catches in the yard and went around to pubs and hotels as far as Windermere. While they were on shift, great granny Nellie tended to the stake net and she sold the fish to neighbours from their backyard or went door to door. when further regulations came in on licencing and restrictions, they decided to call it a day and both boats slowly rotted away.

| two |

GLOSSARY

BABBY or BARN – Baby.

BAR - A long Sandbank at the mouth of a river.

BANK - A Sandbank, a deposit of sand forming a shallow area in the sea or river.

BED - The bottom of the sea or river, used to describe an area of ground, worm bed, mussel bed, etc.

BENT - Name for grass that grows amongst the sand dunes (Marram grass).

BRACK - Breaking sand on the edge of a sandbank, where water is undermining it causing it to crack.

BROB/ BROG - A piece of wood used to mark a safe route across the sands.

CAFF SAND - Soft sand deposited on top of a sandbank, where footprints sink deep. See LILLY SAND.

CHANNEL - A large and deep waterway, usually a rivers main route to the sea.

CRAM - A three pronged tool used mainly to pick up cockles, of Viking origin.

EBB - The tide going out.

FLOOD - The tide coming in.

FOXFIRE – Green bioluminescence or phosphorescence glow created by algae in shallow water at night when disturbed.

GULLEY – A washed out hollow created by water running off a sandbank.

GUT – Large, big, great.

GUTTER – A washed out hollow created by fresh water entering the shore, usually from a stream or beck.

HAWS – Old word to describe sand dunes. E.g. Sandscale Haws, Haverigg Haws, etc.

HEN PENNY – Thin Tellin (Macomangulas tenuis), a small sea shell, usually pink or yellow in colour.

HOLE – A large place of nearly constant deep water when the tide is out. E.g. Pier Hole, Scarth Hole, etc.

LAAL/LARL – Small, tiny.

LILLY SAND – Dry loose sand that gets blown about by the wind, forms CAFF SAND on sand banks.

LONGLINE/ BANKLINE – A line with baited fishing hooks, set on sandbanks for fishing.

MELGRAVE – A hollow scoured out on the edge of a channel bed, usually containing water and quicksand if low in the channel.

MIRE – To sink into the sand.

POOL – A watercourse of a small river, similar to a gutter .e.g. Kirkby Pool, Haverigg Pool. Also a large puddle.

PUNT – A name given to small rowing boats.

RIDDLE – A sieve used for cockles or shrimp.

RUN – The flow of the water.

SCAR – Large areas of stone and gravel in the intertidal areas. e.g. Wortbrig Scar.

SEA PIES – Oystercatchers (Haematopus) sea birds.

SHORE – Land along the edge of a sea, term commonly used instead of beach.

STAKE NET – A net set on the sands for catching fish, fixed to wooden stakes.

An example of Lilly sand blowing in the wind at Askam Pier.
(Kevin Alexander collection).

| three |

A LIST OF SHIPWRECKS

This list is not a fully comprehensive one and does not include small craft like yachts or fishing boats. As you can imagine there are probably a lot more wrecks that simply were not recorded or that have just been forgotten about over time, but these are ones I've come across regarding ships and some of their stories on how they became shipwrecks are recorded in the following pages.

540 - UNKNOWN - Reputedly, Saint Patrick was aboard and shipwrecked. (J.P. Mannex 1849).

1764 - MOLLY
1803 - PROVIDENCE
1810 - HAPPY RETURN
1817 - KINGSMOOR
1821 - PERSERVERANCE
1823 - UNKNOWN
1853 - DUNDALK
1853 - EMERALD
1854 - MARGARET
1858 - HOPE
1858 - FRIENDSHIP
1859 - ABRAMS
1867 - MARY ANNE
1878 - UNKNOWN
1904 - ARIEL
1917 - CONISTON
1946 - ANASTASI
1974 - ACTION

| four |

SHIPWRECKS AND TRAGEDIES

Unfortunately, the Duddon Sands has been the setting for many tragedies over the years. Sadly, there are what seems to be an endless number of accounts that I have come across of loss of life, whether it was from folk who attempted to cross the sands, to bathing incidents or boating accidents, to shipwrecks.

The fact is, the Duddon Estuary was and remains a dangerous place. There are many hidden dangers to be found and many still find themselves in trouble today. Thankfully in this modern age, there are fewer attempts to cross the sands and a lot fewer people using the estuary than in times gone by with regards to bathing and boating and ships do not venture near the Duddon Bar anymore with the loss of the iron mines and ironworks. Also now, folk can call on the services of the Coastguard and two local inshore rescues when in need - the Duddon Inshore Rescue, at Askam, which was founded in 1969, and Haverigg Inshore Rescue founded in 1973. Without these volunteer organisations, many more tragedies would no doubt have occurred.

Whitehaven News, 31st October 1867.

WRECK OFF THE DUDDON. SUPPOSED LOSS OF ALL HANDS.

About one o'clock on Sunday morning, a schooner was observed off the Duddon with a flag of distress flying. About half an hour afterwards she struck on what is known to seamen as the "Duddon Spit", which runs out seawards for a distance of about four miles. The crew, five in number, took to the rigging, and after remaining in this position for about an hour, they came down and got a boat out. At that time a very heavy swell came on, and neither men nor boat were seen afterwards. There can be little doubt that the unfortunate seamen have found a watery grave. The vessel proved to be the Mary Ann, of Glasgow, laden with coals. It is expected she will become a total wreck.

Millom Gazette, 7th September 1904.

A VESSEL WRECKED NEAR HAVERIGG. NARROW ESCAPE OF THE CREW.

The Ariel, a 40-ton towing lighter, of Liverpool, was wrecked off Haverigg Point on Tuesday night. Capt. M'Neish, the owner, along with the Engineer J. Fitzpatrick, left Lytham at 10.30 on Tuesday, fine weather being experienced till they reached Fleetwood where it began to blow and rain. The wind increased and blew very severely when they were opposite Barrow. Capt. McNeish was making for the Clyde, but in consequence of rough weather it was seen that there was no prospect of getting there. To make matters worse, when the outer Duddon buoy was reached the vessel sprung a leak, and the tide being low there was no chance of getting up the Duddon. Seeing the breakers close at hand, the only thing was to escape by the boat, and this was lowered not without considerable difficulty. In fact had there been a delay of only two minutes more there was some question of the men escaping with their lives. They, however, got ashore between Silecroft and Layriggs Road End. The flood tide carried the vessel higher up on the beach. The vessel is insured, and a Liverpool Salvage co., was expected to get the vessel off yesterday (Thursday). After reaching land the two seamen made for Haverigg where they found accommodation for the night. Captain McNeish had only recently purchased the vessel. The Ariel has gone down in deep water in the channel, and may interfere with vessels coming to Millom Piers. It is, however expected that she will be raised by the Salvage Co., though a good deal of damage may have been done by the rough seas.

To this day the wreck still exists not that far from Haverigg Point, and is known locally as "McNally's Wreck" reputably named after a scrap metal dealer who was unsuccessful in salvaging the vessel.

Millom Gazette, 7th September 1917.

SCHOONER WRECKED OFF HAVERIGG. ALL ABOARD PERISH.

A pathetic tragedy of the sea occurred at the entrance of the Duddon Channel on Sunday morning last, during a strong westerly gale, when the schooner 'Coniston' which was owned by the Hodbarrow Mining Company, sank, and her crew (consisting of three men) perished. It is also supposed that a young lady relative of the skipper's was onboard, coming to Millom for a short holiday. The schooner was returning from Bray, Ireland with a cargo of timber, and experienced a heavy gale in the Irish Sea. Upon entering the Duddon Channel she was seen to be in a helpless condition, her masts having been swept away, and preparations were being made to send out for help when she suddenly disappeared from view upon reaching Haverigg. A strong sea was running, and the tide was at the highest experienced for a considerable time. A sharp lookout was kept for any survivors, but none were observed. The small boat, with which an effort might have been made to reach the shore, seems to have been smashed, though it is doubtful if the crew had the opportunity of launching it they could of got off, as the Vessel seems to have turned turtle before anything could be done by those on the boat to help themselves or get assistance from shore.

When the tide had ebbed, no sign was found of the schooner, but later on it was discovered she had been carried by the tide down the Channel on to a sandbank almost a mile away. Five men put out in a boat, and they found the vessel had turned turtle, The tide left her dry, but efforts to right her proved unavailing, and as darkness was setting in the men left her. The schooner was in charge of Captain Dunn, his father, and an able seaman formed the crew, but no sign of them could be seen, and it was not until Tuesday that the bodies of the men were washed ashore at Haverigg.

Haverigg boats Mary Ellen, Audrey, Merry Maid, Sunbeam, Mavis and Thistle. circa 1920.
(Courtesy of John Jeffery and family, Haverigg).

The Coniston was built at Ulverston over 40 years ago, and during that period had done good work for the Hodbarrow Mining Co. The unfortunate vessel and skipper were well known. In selecting the time to sail from Ramsey to Millom the captain was very unfortunate, as bad weather was experienced in the passage across. This is the third Hodbarrow vessel that has been lost since the war commenced. A few years ago, Captain Jones, a well-known Millomite, lost his life off the coast of Scotland in the Bessie Arnold, that vessel foundering in a gale during the Christmas holidays with all on board, including another Millomite and a young fellow who also came from the same port which the crew of the Coniston belonged to.

THE INQUESTS.

Mr. W. T. Lawrence, coroner, held an inquest at the Harbour Hotel on Wednesday morning upon the three bodies of the crew, which had been washed ashore and removed to the hotel. Mr. Fox was foreman of the jury. Mr. S. Wilson represented the owners of the schooner, the Hodbarrow Mining Company, and inspector Huck was also present.

IDENTIFICATION OF THE BODIES.

Captain Edmondson, master of the tugboat at Hodbarrow, was the first witness called. He said he knew the three members of the crew-William Dunn, Joseph Dunn, and Joseph O'Toole, and he identified the bodies the jury just viewed of the three men. He was well acquainted with them, and identified them by their features, which were quite recognisable. William Dunn was the master of the schooner Coniston, which was one of the Hodbarrow fleet of boats and was about 145 tons. He was 20 years of age. Joseph Dunn being the mate, and was 70 odd years of age, whilst Joseph O'Toole was an able seaman of the same boat. Witness last saw them alive on the 25th June at the Bar Buoy in the Duddon Estuary, and was then parting company with them after taking them out with the tug. They had not been to the Duddon since. Witness was expecting them to arrive at the Duddon, but not that morning. When he parted from them on June 25th they were going to Ayr, from whence intended to go to Bray, in Ireland. He was expecting them from Bray, but they called at Ramsey, Isle of Man, on account of the bad weather, and came on from there bound for Millom. Witness did not see the schooner on Sunday morning, but saw the wreck afterwards. The Coniston was laden with timber, and had a deck cargo.

The Coroner: How is it that the Coniston is in charge of such a young sailor?

Witness: I cannot say.

How long has he been master? - Nearly two years.

Joseph Dunn was his father? -Yes, sir.

Had he ever been master? -I cannot say, he has been at sea all his life.

Was Wm. Dunn an Able young fellow? -yes.

Was he a good seaman? -Yes, so far as I know he was.

Joseph Dunn, the father, was also a man of experience? -yes, he had great experience, had the old man.

What do you say about O'Toole? - I don't know much about him.

How many in the crew had the Coniston? - Three when she left here on the 25th June.

Mr Wilson said the Captain was a master before he was put in charge of the Coniston, and was master of a much larger boat previously. He had every confidence in the young fellow, or he would not of put him in charge of the boat.

FINDING THE BODIES.

Harry Hoskin (18), rope lad at Hodbarrow Mines, who resides in Haverigg, stated that on Tuesday morning, about 6 o'clock, he was on the shore near bar sandbank, when he saw the body of a man lying face downwards in a hole, between Haverigg and Silecroft, and was half-covered with water. He noticed the face was badly bruised and covered in blood. He caught hold of him and dragged him on to the dry sand, and then gave information to the police. The body was that of a man about 20 years of age, and apparently a sailor, He saw the body searched by P.C. Whiteside, and in the pockets of the deceased were found a knife, a pencil, three halfpence in copper, an empty purse, and a harbour note from Ramsey.

P.C. Whiteside handed in the articles found on the body.

The Coroner: This note is a receipt for harbour dues.

Edward Burt, coal miner, Chenterley street, Durham, at present spending a holiday at Haverigg, said he was a native of the village, and on Tuesday morning he found a body on Duddon Bar. He first noticed a big heap of what he thought was seaweed, but on investigation he found it was the body of a man. The time would be about 7-45 am. He signalled to some men who were about 250 yards away, nearer Haverigg and who were standing by the other body which had been found. The second body was that of a sailor about 70 years of age, and he identified it as that of Joseph Dunn. Witness had known him for a good many years. On Sunday witness was on the shore, and saw the Coniston in the Duddon Estuary. He did not see her sailing, she had capsized in the Channel. He knew it was the Coniston. The sea was very rough, and a strong breeze was blowing, from the west. Upon examining the body, he found a finger on the hand almost severed, and there was a deep wound on one temple. He assisted in removing the body to where the first body was laying, and it was afterwards removed to the Harbour Hotel, Haverigg.

A Juror asked how did witness know the boat was the Coniston, if it had turned over before he saw it?

Witness said there was away of picking out these boats, and he distinguished the Coniston by the cross trees.

The Coroner said that matter was not of much importance, as they now knew the vessel was the Coniston.

John Butcher, miner, residing at Haverigg, stated that on Tuesday afternoon he was on the shore near No. 5 buoy in the Channel at low water mark, and found the dead body of a man , a sailor, lying face downwards , and the body appeared to have been recently washed up; the tide had just left. The body appeared to be that of a man between 27 and 30 years of age, and had been identified as Joseph O'Toole. There was a mark over the left eye. Witness gave information to the police, and was present when the body was searched, but nothing was found upon him.

This was the whole of the evidence.

The Coroner, in summing up, said to his mind the verdict was perfectly clear. They knew the circumstances very well. The Coniston was attempting to get into the Duddon, and capsized in that attempt. They knew the crew had disappeared, and the bodies viewed by the jury had been identified as those of the crew of the schooner. Although in their own minds they may feel what was the cause of death, yet the evidence showed that the three men were found on the shore. Their deaths might be due to the capsizing of the vessel, which was loaded with timber, or they might have been struck and killed, in which case drowning would not be the cause of death, but the jury would be safe in bringing in a verdict that the men were found drowned, and to all appearances they were drowned by the wreck of the Coniston.

THE VERDICT.

Thee Foreman said the jury were unanimous in their verdict of 'Found Drowned'. He wished to express, on behalf of the jury and himself sympathy with the relatives.

WASHED UP BY THE SEA. WOMAN'S DEAD BODY FOUND AT WALNEY.

An Inquest was held at the Barrow Police Court on Wednesday morning on the dead body of a woman unknown, who was found lying on the beach at South-end, Walney, on Monday morning.

Mr. George Harrison, South End Farm, Walney, spoke to seeing the body of a woman lying on the beach at 7 am.

P.S. Postlethwaite said he received the body. The young woman was but scantily attired, and around the neck was a small gold locket and chain containing a photograph of herself and a young man. The body did not appear to have been in the water a very long time. A schooner was wrecked off Millom on Sunday morning. He had made inquiries and ascertained there was a lady on board.

Coroner F. W. Poole: In all probability she is the woman who was seen on this boat. She may be identified later.

A verdict of 'Found Drowned' was returned.

THE CONISTON REMOVED.

Steam tugs had been engaged upon the work of raising the wrecked schooner each day since Sunday, and on Wednesday afternoon a successful attempt was made, and the Coniston was brought with the tide on to the Duddon Sands between Hodbarrow Point and Millom Pier. She showed signs of having encountered heavy gales. On Thursday morning a number of workmen were engaged in making an aperture into the side of the vessel to effect an entrance into the cabin, as it was thought possible the body of the captains sister might be discovered there'n. Whilst at work, the men received word that the body of the woman washed ashore on the south end of Walney Island on Monday morning had been identified as that of the young lady who was a passenger on the ill-fated Coniston, and the men immediately ceased operations.

RELATIVES IDENTIFY BODIES.

Mrs. Dunn, mother of the deceased captain, accompanied by her daughter and another relative, arrived in Millom from Ireland on Wednesday afternoon. They proceeded to Haverigg, and Mrs.

Dunn identified the bodies which had been washed ashore as those of her husband, son, and a relative. On Thursday she identified the body left by the tide on Walney Island on Monday as that of her daughter Kathleen Dunn, 22 years of age, who was a passenger on board the Coniston, and was intending to have a short holiday in Millom. The body was brought to Millom this morning for interment this afternoon along with the bodies of her father and brother.

A BODY STILL MISSING.

There is still another body missing, that of a youth named Thomas Redmond, of Summer hill Wicklow, a cousin of the late Miss Dunn.

The wreck of the Coniston still exists and lies just off of Hodbarrow Point to this day, and occasionally gets uncovered by the shifting sands.

Lancaster Gazette, 16th November 1878.

On Friday last Captain Myers, of Scott- street, Barrow, went to Millom for the purpose of bringing a 20ft. open boat to Barrow, together with some boxes of furniture, which it was intended to ship to Ireland by the Belfast boat. He was joined by his brother-in-law, Timothy Birkett, who lives at Haverigg. They left the Duddon about eleven o'clock at night, at which time there was half a gale of wind blowing, and a nasty sea running. They should have reached Barrow in a few hours, but as they did not arrive some apprehension was felt for their safety. It was not till Monday that Mr Bird, fisherman, found the dead body of Birkett on the sands, and it was then thought the boat must have been swamped, and the two men drowned. Since then the boat has been washed up on Walney Island, along with some of the boxes and utensils it contained. The body of Myers has not been found, although search has been made. He was captain of the Helen Mar, a schooner owned by Mr J. Ashcroft, now lying in the docks at Barrow, and he was married and had a family. An inquest at Askam Hotel on Wednesday, when a verdict of "Found drowned" was returned. We heard last night that Myers father-in-law saw them leave Millom at eleven o'clock, and that the furniture they were carrying was for a brother-in-law at Belfast.

Soulby's Ulverston Advertiser, 31st October 1867.

DEATH BY DROWNING ON DUDDON SANDS.

An inquest was held on Monday afternoon, at the house of Mr Thos. Gawith, farmer, Ronhead, near Dalton, before Wm. Butler, Esq, coroner, on the veiw of the bodies of James and John Bird, fishermen, Ronhead-foot, aged respectably 19 and 16 years, who were drowned on Duddon under the following circumstances; -John Bird, fisherman, said – Deceased were my sons and went out to fish for flukes on Friday night last, in company with Wm. Allison. I was expecting them to return Saturday morning, and was looking out for them with a spy-glass. About 8am. I saw them leave Hodbarrow. When about half way across towards Ronhead side, I saw the boat was very heavily laden. -Henry Bird, brother of deceased, deposed that on Saturday morning last he trimmed the boat, and set them off from Hodbarrow side. The boat was heavily laden, and he told them to be very careful. -The jury, returned a verdict of Death of drowning, due to the unsettling of the boat in the Duddon estuary. The body of Allison had not yet been found.

Millom Gazette, 26th August 1904.

DROWNED IN CROSSING THE DUDDON.

Towards evening on Saturday a man named Albert Walker, of Newton-street, Millom, was drowned whilst crossing the Duddon estuary from Kirkby to Millom. Walker, who along with many others had been attending Kirkby Flower Show, set off to cross the sands to Millom, in company with a man named Hill. The stationmaster at Kirkby, Mr. Fox, knowing the tide was rising, and knowing the great danger the men were running, endeavoured to persuade them from going, but Walker would listen to no advice, and crossed onto the Green, across the Kirkby Pool, and then went in the direction of Millom. The tide was making fast at the time, and he had quite a mile and a half of water to face. He could be seen splashing in the water as he walked through it. Three men, named Edgar, Norton, and Stones, went after him, but the tide enveloped Walker and carried him away. Search was made for him, but it was not till 4 o'clock on Sunday morning that the dead body was found, left by the tide, by George Fell, of Kirkby. The body was conveyed to the Ship Hotel, Kirkby.

THE INQUEST

An inquest was held at the Ship Inn, Kirkby-in-Furness, on Monday evening, before Mr. Coroner Poole, Mr. Joseph Coulton being the foreman of the jury.

Wm. Hill, Newton-street, Millom, said the deceased resided at 127, Newton-street, Millom, was a brick layer's labourer, and was 21 years of age. On Saturday last witness and deceased left

Millom by the 3.18 train for Kirkby. On arriving there they called at the Railway Inn, and had some beer.

The Coroner; How much?- I don't know.

How many pints?- I can't remember.

Were you so drunk you can't remember?- I was not drunk.

How much had you?- Couple of pints.

Was he drunk?- He had more than me.

Witness, continuing, said they left the Railway Inn and went to the Ship Inn, where witness had a small rum, and deceased had two pints of beer.

Did you come here to spend most of your time in a public-house?- Nearly. He left Walker at the station, as he refused to go by train, saying he would go across the sands.

Were you drunk as well?- No, sir.

But he was drunk?- Yes.

Why did you leave him. You knew he was not fit to go across the sands?- I tried to keep him back, but he shoved me off.

That is the greater reason you should have followed him. Where did you last see him?- Going across the Marsh.

What public-house were you last in?- The "Ship".

Edward P. Fox, stationmaster at Kirkby, said he saw the deceased at the station about five o'clock, at which time he was helplessly drunk. He was misbehaving himself, and two of his companions took him in hand, but owing to his jostling he pushed a young lady on the line. He returned in about fifteen minutes, and witness told him to lie down. He replied 'can't get across the sands tonight,' and witness replied that he was not in a fit condition to cross.

A train for Askam came in, and after it had gone out witness went to see where deceased was, and found he had started to cross the sands. Witness drew Hill's attention to the danger the deceased was going into, but he made an indifferent reply. Witness spoke to others about the man, but they ridiculed the idea of his being drowned, and said when he got into the water it would soon waken him up. Witness watched him through a pair of field glasses, and saw him in the water splashing, but he did not appear to be over the knees. Witness had to go and attend to a train, and when he looked again, the man had disappeared. Three young men then set off to look for him, and they traced his footsteps.

By the Coroner; The tide was in and the place is full of holes.

Then he could not get across?- No, he could not even if he had been sober.

Was Hill drunk; He was under the influence of drink, but not so bad as Walker.

But did he know what he was doing?- No, he hardly knew what he was doing.

Was there no one you could have got to look after him?- Well we had an extraordinary traffic that afternoon; we were taxed to the utmost, and had a level crossing to look after. The platform was crowded with people, watching him.

Geo. Fell said he found the body of the deceased at five o'clock on Sunday morning on Duddon Sands.

In reply to the Coroner, the constable said the watch on the body had stopped, but owing to the movement of the body it had started again.

The witness Fell said there was a hole a yard leap where the body was found.

The Coroner in summing up, said this is the second inquest he had held where a Millom man had gone out of his own district to get drunk. It seemed that the deceased and Hill came over to Kirkby to spend practically the whole of the time in a public-house. There was no doubt that both of them had a good deal to drink. Hill was probably nearly as bad as the deceased, and hardly knew what he was doing, otherwise he (the Coroner) would have had something severe to say to him about leaving his companion in such a condition. He was probably very little more responsible for his actions than the deceased himself. If the deceased had any knowledge of what he was doing he would never have attempted to make his way across the sands at full tide.

There was nothing that he (the Coroner) could do to prevent men making fools of themselves and losing their lives in the way this man had done.

The jury could only find a verdict that the deceased was drowned whilst attempting to cross the sands whilst under the influence of drink. It was exceedingly sad that men should throw their lives away and make beasts of themselves in the way the deceased and his companion had done. The jury returned a verdict in accordance with the Coroners suggestion.

Kirkby-in-Furness Railway station.
(From the Sankey collection. Copyright Cumbria Archives).

Haverigg from the sands.
(From the Sankey collection. Copyright Cumbria Archives).

Millom Gazette, 8th June 1923.

BOATING TRADEGY OFF HAVERIGG.   FIVE LIVES LOST IN DUDDON DISASTER.

Two men and two lads belonging to Haverigg and a Millom man lost their lives as a result of a shocking tragedy which occurred on Sunday afternoon. The sailing boat "Agnes" was returning to Haverigg from Barrow when she sank during the struggle with an adverse wind, and the five lives she carried were lost. The names of the those onboard were;-

Henry Dooley (35) an iron miner, Concrete Square, Haverigg.
William Foster (35) gas works labourer, Concrete Square, Haverigg.
James Grenfell (28) gas works labourer, 54 Lonsdale Road, Millom.
John Thomas Dooley (15) unemployed, Concrete Square, Haverigg.
Edward Kendall (15) newsboy, Concrete Square, Haverigg.

The boat, which had been recently acquired by Mr. Henry Dooley, and was in his charge, was a vessel of about 20 feet in length, carrying a mainsail and a jibsail. It left Barrow at a quarter to two on Sunday afternoon, and proceeded down the 'Meetings' and Scarth Channel. It then fought its way in the teeth of the wind to a point where it could avoid the sandbank and turn back into the wind, making for home. The ebb tide probably necessitated its course being further out than usual. Meanwhile, its passage was being watched from the shore at Haverigg by several persons. They saw the vessel tacking carefully skilfully, when suddenly, apparently struck by a squall, it heeled over, rising at the bow, and disappeared. The horror-stricken watchers raised the alarm at once, and Mr. W. Mellon speedily had his own boat moored and went to the rescue. It was all to no purpose- no trace could be found of any survivor. Nor was any definitive evidence of the tragedy forth coming until nearly midnight, when boats in charge of Messrs. Metters and Sage came up to Haverigg on the flowing tide and made it known they had found the lost vessel on a sandbank. And in Mr. Sage's boat reposed the body of James Grenfell. All were lingering _ to the fate of the ill-starred crew were now dispelled, and Haverigg and Millom people knew that a fearful tragedy had stricken the community. The search was continued with unflagged vigilance, but no further success came to the boats. On Monday, however, the bodies of William Foster and John Thomas Dooley (nephew to Henry Dooley, who had charge of the "Agnes") were found on the shore at Walney. On Wednesday the body of Henry Dooley was found on Walney.

STORY OF THE TRAGEDY

Henry Dooley has for a long time been accredited one of the most expert boatmen in Haverigg. He was owner of the yacht "Maud," but some months ago decided to dispose of her, as being too large for his purpose. He accordingly came to an arrangement with Mr. Henry Newton of Barrow, the outcome of which was that the two men agreed to exchange boats. Mr. Newton was to take possession of "Maud," and Mr. Dooley was to acquire the "Agnes." It was also agreed to effect the exchange at Whitsuntide, but at that season it was found that the weather was altogether, unsuitable for sailing, and the deal was not carried out. On Saturday the weather was summerlike, and Mr. Dooley decided to make the trip to Barrow in the "Maud" and return in the "Agnes." As the sail was likely to be a most enjoyable one in such pleasant weather conditions, Mr. Dooley took five friends with him. On the way across they encountered Mr. Newton, who had been coming to Haverigg on somewhat similar errand, but on learning Mr. Dooleys purpose, the owner of the "Agnes" put about and accompanied the "Maud" to Barrow. One of the Haverigg yachts passengers was Mr. George Rodda, 12 Oak Terrace, Leasingthorne, Durham, who was on a visit to Haverigg. He had not definitely intended to remain overnight and sail back on Sunday, as the others meant to do, and when Mr. Dooley expressed the opinion that the five passengers would be sufficient for the "Agnes," he at once determined to return to Millom by train. To this decision Mr. Rodda, in all probability, owes his life.

BOAT ENCOUNTERS SQUALLS.

On the fatal Sunday Mr. Newton saw his friend Dooley off from Barrow, the time being about quarter to two. The "Agnes," with the five men onboard, went speeding out towards the estuary, and it was not until she ran into the Scarth channel that she met the full force of the wind. Mr. Dooley had assured Mr. Newton that if he found it too stormy to make a reasonably safe crossing he would return. The former owner of the ill-fated boat watched the craft with some misgiving as she ran into the wind, but when she did not turn back he assumed that it would make the passage safely, for he had absolute faith in the Haverigg mans judgement and seamanship. The boat was not again seen at Barrow.

In normal conditions the "Agnes" ought to have made Haverigg little after three, but her progress was considerably impeded by the frequent squalls and the rough water. About that time she was seen from Haverigg beach by men who knew the vessel. She appeared to be well out towards the mouth of the Duddon Estuary, somewhere between buoys Nos. 3 and 4.

Alexander Jeffrey, who was watching from the seafront, tells his story thus; "We watched the boat come along to the bar. The breeze had freshened, and it seemed to much for it. Dooley kept throwing the boat up into the wind to ease it. Then we saw it slip back and disappear." George Rodda, states that he and his companions saw the boat coming under sail towards Haverigg. They happened to turn their eyes from it for a few minutes, and upon on looking could find no trace of it.

THE MIDNIGHT SEARCH.

The end of the "Agnes," or the fact of the disappearance, was received by an old man living at Steel Green, and by several other watchers from the beach and sandhills. Mr. Jeffrey rushed to the house of Mr. W. Mellon, and in a very short time vessels in charge of Mr. Mellon and Mr. R. Wright were out searching the estuary in hope of giving succour to survivors. But it was all to no purpose. The "Agnes" and her costly burden had been swallowed up and left no trace. At low tide the searchers made another effort, this time in small punts or broad-bottomed rowing boats. Amongst those who went out on the search were Messrs. W. and A. Mellon, Mr. S. Sage, Messrs. Wright and Messrs. Metters. With the rising tide, about half past eleven, two boats returned, and one bore the body of James Grenfell. He was revertantly brought ashore and carted to the mortuary, and after identification brought back to his home in Millom. Mr Sage had also stated that the boat had been found on Hardacre Sandbank, turned turtle, and with her mast broken. The search party had righted the boat and made search for the bodies, with result that Grenfell was found about 400 yards away from the "Agnes." A number of vessels had also put out from Barrow, but the tide had flowed over the banks before any further discoveries were made, and the searchers returned to Haverigg and Barrow.

BODIES FOUND AT WALNEY.

On Monday morning Jas. Wade and Jas. Taylor, of Barrow, were line-fishing at the north end of Walney Island when they discovered a body lying in a declivity of the sand, where it had evidently been left by the receding tide. They had heard of the tragedy which had occurred in the Estuary the previous day, and at once connected their discovery with that occurrence. A further search round brought them to a second body, about 200 yards from the first. With the aid of a neighbouring farmer the bodies were taken from the shore and eventually to the mortuary. The first was identified as that of William Foster and the other as that of the boy John Thomas Dooley. On Wednesday morning a body which was identified as that of the elder Dooley was also found on the shores of Walney Island.

IMPRESSIVE SCENES AT HAVERIGG.

Sunday was a cold, windy day, an unpleasant change from the summerlike weather of Saturday. On Haverigg beach the gusty wind caught up the sand after the tide had receded, and made it miserable for walking. Further out, in the Estuary, the water was disturbed and choppy, and the crests of white foam told men of experience that a sailing vessel would have a difficult journey to come round the banks from Walney and make Haverigg. This fact drew a lot of attention to the little sailing vessel which appeared 5 miles out shortly after 3 o'clock, friends who had known Mr. Dooley's intentions had no doubt that the craft coming round the shoals was the "Agnes." Even at a distance of four miles her manoeuvres could be clearly seen with the aid of binoculars, and admiration of the skill with which she was being handled was aroused in the watchers. From first to last, be it noted, Mr. Dooley's handling of his boat has never been brought into question. The breeze was gradually freshening, and it was evident that "Agnes" was repeatably meeting heavy gusts of wind, which are much more dangerous than a steady gale. The gallant little vessel met one of these and then disappeared. News of what had been seen was bruited abroad, and over the quiet of Haverigg's Sunday afternoon came an air of impending tragedy. Those who were setting out for a walk retraced their steps and found their way to the beach. Already two boats had gone to the assistance of "Agnes," and the period of waiting was an exacting one for those on shore.

THE TIME OF WAITING.

Hope sprang uppermost, but at best it was superficial. It was suggested that the vessel had found the passage too heavy, and dropped sail, and turned back into Scarth Channel, but the crowd who most insistently spoke hopefully had little faith in their own suggestions. When the vessels returned, and it was reported that no trace could be found that might suggest a disaster, colour was given to the theory that the "Agnes" had gone back to Barrow. The police then made inquiries by telephone at the Barrow end, and, despite their preparedness for the worst, the report from Barrow came as a shock to the anxious watchers on the windswept shore at Haverigg. The "Agnes" had left Barrow at a quarter to two with five men onboard, and had not returned. Lingering doubts vanished, and half a dozen families knew they had been bereaved. But still there was uncertainty, if the vessel had gone down, surely the search parties would have found an oar, or a cap, or some trace?. So the afternoon dragged away, with interminable coming and going to and from the beach. When the tide was at its lowest a young man who had been searching the sandbank came and told P.C Prentice and others that he could see three objects on Hardacre Bank. A few people confronted his opinion, but the majority could see nothing whatever, however, unwilling to let any opportunity of salvaging the bodies pass, several boatmen launched punts and set off to the spot. For two or three hours the watchers waited in ever-growing suspense, and the sands were trodden as they had never been trodden before.

RECOVERY OF THE FIRST BODY.

Darkness fell, and still there was still no sign from the boats that were out on the estuary. Ever and annon in lurid crimson glow flushed the sky as catching as casting or 'Slagging' operations were carried out at Barrow and Millom, and under the ruddy glare the usually deserted shore presented a strange spectacle. About a hundred people were gathered at the water's edge about a mile and a half from Poolside Channel, and each time the unnatural light filled the sky it showed isolated parties crossing and recrossing the sands. The throng of people on the water mark were being slowly pressed back by the rising tide, when, about twenty past eleven, a light showed from the water about 300 yards off. A murmur went round as it was realised that one of the boats was returning. As the vessel passed the point where the watchers stood, the boatmen exchanged a few words with P.C. Prentice. The latter turned and sent two lads to bring stretchers down to Poolside Channel and the word went round that Grenfell's body had been recovered.

When the boat grounded on the shingle directly opposite Poolside, the throng had emersed the length of the sands. But the body was not in this boat. It was in Simon Sage's vessel, which grounded some five minutes later. The crowd held back, hushed as the body of James Grenfell was brought from the boat and borne up to the mortuary, which stands on the sand banks. The news of the finding of the 'Agnes' and the broken mast gave rise anew to speculation regarding the manner of the accident, but within a short time the crowd dwindled away, and at midnight, the beach was restored to its normal quiet, and left to the rising tide.

THE FIVE VICTIMS.

Henry Dooley was an unmarried man, but he was the sole support of his grandfather, with whom he lived. He was employed at Hodbarrow, he was universally accounted one of the best and most capable seaman in Haverigg. His nephew, Jack Dooley, had not commenced work since leaving school and had not previously made a trip on a sailing boat. He was in high spirits on Saturday, and Mr. Rodda states that he frequently pulled out of his pocket the money his mother had given him and showed it to his companions on the "Maud." The younger Dooley's father has been unemployed for some considerable time. Edward Kendall was the lad of a bright disposition, and had been in the habit of delivering newspapers for Miss Nicholson, of Millom. His father is in America.

James Grenfell was an ex-serviceman. He served with the colours from 1914 to the end of the war, and came through unscathed. He first of all joined the 4th Kings Own, with whom he went to France, but he was later transferred to the labour corps. He was a powerful swimmer, and won the Royal Humane Society's certificate for bravery in 1906. On that occasion Grenfell, a boy of 11 years, dived fully dressed into one of the tidal gullies on the Embankment at Millom, and rescued a little girl who was in danger of drowning. William Foster alone of the five men was a married man, and leaves a widow and two young children. He was an ex-soldier, and was wounded and gassed in the war. He drew a disability pension. Foster is said to have been a strong swimmer.

THE INQUESTS – "ACCIDENTALLY DROWNED" VERDICTS.

An inquiry into the circumstances surrounding the death of James Grenfell, 54 Lonsdale Road, Millom, was conducted in Millom Court Room on Monday by Mr. R. W. Marley, Deputy Coroner for the Lordship of Millom. Thomas Henry Grenfell, iron ore miner, 54 Lonsdale Road, Millom, identified the body found on Sunday night as that of his son, James Grenfell, who had resided with him at 54 Lonsdale Road. Witness stated that he had last seen his son alive on Friday, as he was on a different shift from deceased. He had not known anything about the trip his son was going to make. His son was a good swimmer.

FINDING OF THE BOAT.

Simon Sage, fisherman, 19 Main Street, Haverigg, stated that on Sunday he had heard about the accident that had taken place, and he went down to the channel on the ebb tide at night in a small boat. Continuing witness said, " We found the boat. It was wrong side up, high and dry on the bank. We raised the boat but saw nothing under it. Then we looked further, and found the body on the water edge, about a quarter of a mile away from the boat."

Witness did not know the man whose body they had found, but others in the boat with him knew who it was, and told him it was James Grenfell, of Millom.

Coroner; Was there anything peculiar about the boat?

Witness; The boat was wrong side up and mast was broken.

There was nothing else wrong with it? – No no.

What sort of boat was it? – It was an open boat, about 20 feet long.

You are an experienced boatman. Was it a fair day for people to be coming across from Barrow to Haverigg? – Well, it was a wild day.

Would you consider they were taking a risk? Would you have come yourself? – I think I would have gone back into Barrow myself.

It is a treacherous place this, is it not? – Yes.

Did you know any of the people who were supposed to be in the boat? – Yes, I knew the other four.

They were good boatmen? – One was - Dooley.

Was he an experienced man? – Yes.

Where did you make this find? – On Duddon Bar, south of Buoy No. 4.

Where did you find the body? – A quarter of a mile seaward from the boat.

How would you describe the place? – South Hollow, is the name of the channel.

It is dry at low water? – Well, there are sandbanks all around it.

RODDA'S STORY

George Rodda, presently residing at 31 Poolside, Haverigg, stated that it had been arranged to go across to Barrow on Saturday, and he arranged with Harry Dooley to go.

Coroner; To buy a boat?

Witness; No it was only for the trip that I went.

Deceased went with you amongst others? – Yes.

What time did you get to Barrow on Saturday? – Four o'clock.

Did you have a good passage? - Yes.

Are you a boatman? – No.

Do you know anything about sailing? – No.

Who arranged the boat? – Dooley.

Is he an experienced boatman? – Yes.

Were they going to get another boat? – They were going to come back in another boat. We took the "Maud" and they were coming back with the "Agnes" on Sunday.

You came back to Millom by train on Saturday night? – Yes.

Why didn't you stay? – I never intended staying; I just went for the trip there. And then Mr. Dooley said there were quite sufficient to come back in a smaller boat on the Sunday.

What happened on Sunday? – We were on the shore when she was coming across between three and four o'clock. We saw the boat coming but we were not sure of it, but on account of her coming so far across and pointing to Haverigg we thought it was the "Agnes."

Had it the sails up then? – Yes.

Was it blowing hard at the time? – Yes, it was blowing abit strong.

What happened? – It was sailing alright when we saw it. We turned our eyes away, and then we turned around again, and the boat had disappeared.

It seemed alright when you saw it last? – Yes.

Did you hear Dooley talking about this boat on your journey on Saturday? -No.

He never mentioned it? – We knew he was going for it before, at Whitsuntide, but on account of the bad weather he did not go. Then he thought the weather had picked up, and that he would go Saturday and come back Sunday.

WHAT AN EYE WITNESS SAW.

Alexander Jeffrey, iron ore miner, Concrete Square, Haverigg, said that he and some others were on the sea front at Haverigg, on Sunday. "We watched this boat come along the bar. The breeze had freshened, and it seemed too much for it. Dooley kept throwing the boat up into the wind to ease her. Then we saw it slip back and disappear. The masts were alright then."

Do you know anything about sailing boats? – Yes.

Was this man Dooley sailing this boat properly? – Oh, yes, he was handling the boat all right.

It was simply the weather that upset it? – Yes, the breeze was freshening.

Did you know Grenfell? – Not personally.

Dooley was a good boatman? – Yes, and Foster had been a man accustomed to a boat.

When did you first see the boat? – About three o'clock.

How long was it after that you saw the boat go down? – Threequarters to an hour.

Mr. Sage was recalled and questioned by the Coroner.

Do you think anymore bodies are likely to be found? – Yes, I think so.

Will the tide bring them up? – Yes.

On this side? – No, on the Walney side.

How far is it across? – eight miles.

They were only half way? – Yes.

Did they go round Walney and Peel Island? – No, they came through the channel.

They left Barrow at quarter to two, and they should have been at Haverigg at about three o'clock? – Yes, in ordinary weather, but there was a head wind.

THE VERDICT

Mr. Grenfell said he had no complaint to make, and the Coroner made his verdict as follows ; "It seems to be an exceedingly sad affair. No other words can describe it – five men to lose their lives in a boating accident of this sort. I think there is no doubt how the deceased died, and I am not concerned with the others at present. I find he was accidentally drowned by the capsizing of the boat "Agnes."

The Coroner expressed his sympathy with Mr. Grenfell.

INQUEST AT BARROW.

In the Court Room at Barrow, on Tuesday afternoon, Mr. F. Poole, Coroner of Furness, conducted an inquiry into the circumstances surrounding the death of two men whose bodies were found on Walney on Monday. The remains have been identified as those of William Foster (35) gas works labourer, and John Thomas Dooley (15) unemployed, both of Concrete Square, Haverigg.

Henry Dooley, Concrete Square, Haverigg, stated that he had identified one of the bodies as that of his son, John Thomas Dooley, He had not been put to any trade so far. Witness last saw him alive on Friday, 1st June.

Mrs. Eliza Ellen Foster, 22, Concrete Square, said that the deceased, William Foster, was her husband. She had last seen him alive on Saturday, about one o'clock, when he left Haverigg to go to Barrow on the sailing boat "Maud."

A RISKY BUISNESS.

Henry Newton, plater and engineer, 13a Walney Road, Barrow, said that about 1.30 P.M. on Saturday he set sail from Barrow towards Haverigg for the purpose of exchanging boats with the deceased Henry Dooley. On the way he met Dooley on board the "Maud" and returned to Barrow with him. He spoke over the arrangement with Dooley, and then got his boat, the "Agnes," ready for sea, and landed it over to Dooley. About 1.45 p.m. on Sunday Dooley left Barrow in the "Agnes." He said he would sail through Scarthole, and if it was too bad he would come back and go to Millom by train, and return the following week for the boat. Witness had watched Dooley go down Walney Channel and past Scarthole and then he went home. There were five onboard altogether onboard the "Agnes" but witness did not know any of them by name except Dooley. The "Agnes" was an open sailing boat, cutter rigged, carrying a mainsail and jib, length 20 feet, tonnage 2.31 and drew about 2 feet 4 inches or 2 feet 6 inches. He had known Dooley about four years, and considered him a capable man. He had never known him to run any risk.

Coroner; The "Agnes" was in good condition?

Witness; Yes.

You know these sands very well? – Yes.

I suppose there are a good many sandbanks? – Yes it is all sandbanks between here and the Duddon Buoy. In a big wind or a rough sea it is very bad water.

In a big wind it must be a risky business? – With a lot of sea on it would be hard work.

Has the boat been found? – Yes I have seen her this morning.

Is she smashed up? – Yes, she is broken. The mast is broken and the plates broken. She has been lying on the sands.

Did she capsize. Do you think? – I cannot weigh up how it came about.

Do you know if any of the other men were capable seamen? – I have seen Mr. Foster a few times in a boat, and I take it for granted that he knew a little bit about a boat.

When she left was it your opinion fit to live(leave)? – Well, it was fit to live(leave) providing there was no sea on the sandbanks.

You could not tell that until you got to Scarthole?, you could not tell from where you were? – No. He promised me to sail up Scarthole, and if it was to bad he would come back. I left food for them to have their tea if they came back.

Then you really expected them to come back? – No, but there was a chance. In Dooley's own estimation if he thought it was fit he would go, and if he thought it was too bad he would come back.

OTHER EVIDENCE.

George Rodda repeated the evidence he had given at Millom on the previous day. Alexander Jeffrey also repeated his evidence. James Albert Wade, 15 Ironworks Road, Barrow, said that at 10.a.m. on Monday he was long-line fishing at the northern point of Walney Island. He found the body of a man below the water mark, and about 150 yards away found another body. They procured a cart, with the aid of Mr. Barnes, both bodies were conveyed to North End Farm. They then telephoned to the police, and the bodies were removed to the mortuary. He had heard of the accident in the estuary, and he at once connected the bodies with it. He looked around to see if he could see any others, but he failed.

THE VERDICT.

The Coroner said ; " I find that the deceased man Foster and the boy Dooley were accidentally drowned whilst crossing from Barrow to Millom. The evidence is perfectly clear that the boat had exchanged and were crossing in was in good order when she left Barrow. Dooley was an experienced boatman, and in ordinary weather there is no doubt that he would have been quite safe and made the passage. As the witness Jeffrey says, the wind got up very quickly, and the boat got into difficulties, At the same time the boat seemed to be properly handled. We shall never know, of course, the cause of the boat being swamped, but the fact remains that she was swamped, and that these two, the man and the boy, were unfortunately drowned, also three others lost there lives at the same time."

L to R, John Rowe King, Emily Jeffery (nee King), Ellen George (nee King) and Alexander Jeffery. Concrete Square Haverigg.
(Courtesy of John Jeffery and family, Haverigg).

Soulby's Ulverston Advertiser, 27th August 1874.

THE FATAL ACCIDENT IN THE DUDDON.

On Tuesday the district coroner, John Poole, Esq., held an inquest at the Askam Hotel on the body of John Sandham, aged 26 years, who was drowned on Sunday afternoon, the 16th inst., in the Duddon river.

William Taylor's evidence was to the effect that on the day named, witness, along with John Jones, the deceased John Sandham, Geo. Kellett, Thos. Dixon, John Taylor, Stephen Saunders, and Thos. Taylor, left Askam about 1.30 p.m., rowing to Millom in a boat, and they arrived at the latter place shortly after 2. p.m. The boat was anchored, and the party adjourned to the Devonshire Arms, Holborn Hill. Here the party remained until 4.30 p.m. having during the interval drank five or six half-gallons of ale with a little rum in it. Each of the persons partook of the drink; the deceased was a little affected by the drink, but not so much as some of their number. He was not drunk.

At 4.30 p.m., the party returned and launched the boat, having to drag it, the tide having receded about 12 yards. The whole of them entered the boat, which was rowed down the main channel, no attempt was made to cross, as the tide was ebbing. On arriving opposite Haverigg Point, they found the boat too heavy to float over the shallow water that intervened before they could reach Bird's Hole, and so head right for Askam. They therefore lessened their number by allowing Geo. Kellett, Stephen Saunders, John Taylor, and Thomas Taylor, to leave the boat on the Askam side of the channel, these parties intended to walk home over the sands. Witness and deceased got out of the boat and pushed the boat of the sandbank. Scarcely had they got into the boat she again struck another small sand bank. Sandham jumped out by himself at the bows of the boat, the stem having grounded. Witness did not see deceased, as he was sitting at the stern with his back to him; but John Jones, who was at the bow, saw Sandham push the boat off, without retaining his hold. The boat left deceased, and Jones called out to witness, "Jacks away from the boat; pull around Taylor!" Witness who was holding an oar, pulled the boat around towards deceased, who was about six or seven yards from the boat, and attempting to swim towards it as it was being rowed to him. There was a strong flow of the tide towards Haverigg. After witness had pulled a few strokes, Jones shouted, "He's going down," and deceased instantly disappeared. Witness asked where deceased had sunk, and Jones pointed at the channel about six yards from the boat. Witness jumped out of the boat, expecting Sandham would rise again. Witness could not touch the bottom with his feet, nor did he see the deceased again. The bank was very steep into the channel, and was full of holes. It would require 20 feet of water in the channel before the bank was covered. Deceased was too far off to be reached an oar out. All the men could have come across to Askam after passing the channel. When Jones cried out that Jack had gone down, witness's father (John Taylor), who had left the boat previously, swam out to her. The party in the boat intended to keep within the channel until they reached Bird's hole -(*see glossary. It was located close to Roanhead Crag and no longer exists 2023*), when it would have been easy to row to Askam. When the former lot came across the sands they found one of their number lying on the bank; he might have been asleep, he could not say. This man was lying down had a bottle of drink in his pocket when he left them.

John Jones, a miner of Askam, said that the evidence given by the last witness was correct as far as it had been read to him namely, up to the launching of the boat. His evidence went to show that they came down the main channel, and landed four men, in order to lighten the boat. After striking the first bank Taylor and Sandham got out and pushed the boat off. After continuing between 100 and 200 yards, the boat struck a second time. Deceased got over the bows and shoved her off by pressing his open hands against it; the boat left him, he never having got in her again. Deceased was up to the knees in water. The water was a foot or two depth when the boat struck. Deceased walked after the boat until he was up to the waist, and when between six and seven yards from the boat attempted twice by swimming to reach her. Deceased never spoke. Witness told Taylor to pull around and take deceased up. Taylor pulled as hard as possible, and Sandham was up to the neck in water and went down. Witness thought that when deceased sunk his feet were taken away from him by the strong ebb tide. Witness saw nothing more of deceased after he disappeared.

Tyrus Cleasby, of Haverigg, labourer and fisherman, spoke of finding the body about 6 p.m. on Monday evening, near the side of No. 5 buoy, two miles southwest of Haverigg, when the tide was flowing in the channel. Witness had seen the body about two p.m. floating with the ebb tide, but could not get a boat launched then. He was about 200 yards away when he saw something floating which he thought looked like the body of a man, and he suspected it was that of the deceased. He watched for its return at the flow and found it. Deceased was dressed in trousers, waistcoat and boots, having no coat on. There were no marks of violence on discernible.

The coroner remarked that on a number of occasions in which cases of accidental drowning had occurred, the general rule was that that they had been caused directly or indirectly by drink. He thought, had been told, and hoped that this unfortunate case would prove an exception, but he was sorry it had not. It was quite evident that nearly all, if not all, had got to much drink. Deceased, in pushing off the boat, ought to have retained his hold of her, instead of of which he let the boat go from him. Not only this, but instead of standing until the boat could be turned around and brought up to him, in order that he might get in, he very foolishly followed the boat into the channel. Although trying to swim, it did not appear that he was off his feet. The tide, which was ebbing with great force, took him off his feet, and he was seen no more. There remained, no doubt, deceased was accidentally drowned.

The jury returned a verdict of "Accidentally drowned."

Haverigg Pool.
(From the Sankey collection. Copyright Cumbria Archives).

Millom Gazette, 3rd July 1903.

SAD DROWNING CASE AT HAVERIGG.   THE INQUEST.

On Monday afternoon, at the Harbour Hotel, Haverigg, an inquest was held by Dr. Stoney and a jury into the death of a child, named Thomas Slater Gillbanks, three years of age, son of Myles Gillbanks, miner, Haverigg, who was drowned on Haverigg sands on Saturday Morning. The inquest had been fixed for two o'clock, but Dr. Stoney was detained at Hodbarrow Hospital attending to an accident case until a long time past that hour, and it was not until after three o'clock, that the twelve "good men and true" who had been summoned to assist him, and were anxiously awaiting his arrival by the banks of Haverigg Pool, ___ worthy Doctor to arrive.

The Jury was as follows; Messers T. J. C. Fox, Wm. North, James Doughty, Wm. Hill, Ed. R. Ottley, P. Strike, John Newby, W. G. Metters, James Gendle, Wm. Brown, Wm. Park, Thomas Parrott.

Mr. T. J. C. Fox was elected foreman of the jury. Mr. Newby asked if it was necessary for all the jury to view the body?.

The Coroner said the body would have to be seen by each of the jurymen.

The jury then preceded to view the body.

The first witness was Myles Gillbanks, who said he lived at 31 Silverdale, Haverigg, and worked as a miner at Hodbarrow. He identified the body viewed by the jury as that of his son Thomas Slater Gillbanks, who was three years of age. He last saw the child alive at 10 o'clock on Saturday morning. Deceased was then playing about the house. About half an hour afterwards, said witness, they came and told ___ he was in the Pool.

Christina Crellin, said she lived at 16, Bank End, with her husband, Thomas Crellin, who worked at Hodbarrow Mines. Last Saturday morning she came out of the house at about 11 o'clock to see after a young dog that had ran out of the house. She looked down at the waterside and saw four children in danger. She saw one of the children tumble into the water. She shouted to her husband, but he did not hear her, and witness ran down to the waterside to get them out. Two men, Richard Edger and Joseph Wayman, ran past her, and Richard Edger handed one of the children out to witness and fetched another out. Wayman got the third child out and then ran down the embankment to see if he could see the other child, but he could not see it, as it had sunk.

The Coroner; Who went to look for the fourth child/ - Witness; Wayman and Edger both jumped into the water where I had told them it had gone it, but they could not find it. Wayman looked along the poolside near the sewer, which was a dangerous place, but they saw nothing more of the child.

A Juryman; Did all four children fall in into the water? – Witness; No, only one.

What made the other three go in? – They were standing on the sewer wall by Poolside and the tide was coming in fast. Another three minutes and they would of all been drowned.

The Foreman; Then the other children were in the water, but not in the Pool ___.

The Coroner; You saw the deceased slip off the wall? – He slipped fast and fell.

How old were the elder children? – The oldest of them would be about five.

And there was no one else with them?- No.

When you got the other children out, the water was nearly up to their knees, and the tide was coming in fast? – Yes.

James Wright said; I live at 36 Concrete Square, Haverigg, and work at Hodbarrow as a miner. On Saturday morning I was down teaming the water out of a boat at about 10 o'clock. I saw people rushing on the beach and I went to see what was the matter. I found that a child was in the water. A man called Richard Burt was getting a net ready, and I assisted him to look for the body. After that I sent up for my own net and used that. I found the body of a child – the deceased. I found the body about 25 yards away from the Harbour Hotel, about 300 yards from where he fell in. There was about five foot of water when I got there, about an hour after he fell into the water.

A Juryman; I suppose you dragged the body up in the net? – Yes.

The Juryman; You would hardly be able to tell where you picked it up.

Richard Edger said; I live at 25 Main- Street, Haverigg, and am a labourer working with Aird's (*Hodbarrow Sea wall builder*). On Saturday morning I was at home, having knocked off work in consequence of the rain. I went to have a walk on the banks at about a quarter to 11, and I and Joseph Wayman stood by the end of the schools talking. I heard three little lads shouting. I looked at them and never took any heed of what they were doing, but when I looked again they were standing up to their knees in water. I called to Wayman, and we both ran down and when we got to them one of the children said, "There's our Tom in the water." Wayman went past them to see if he could see this one that was lost and while he was going down I picked one of the children up and carried him out of the water and gave him to Mrs. Crellin. Then I went back again and fetched another and put him on the side. I went back again and jumped in to try and find the one that was missing.

The Coroner; What became of the other? – Wayman brought of out. I could not find anything of the missing child.

What depth of water was there? – Up to the waist. There was a good three feet.

Did you see the body brought up? – Yes, sir.

By whom? – James Wright.

Did you know the child? – yes, sir I know it was Tom, That was all.

The Coroner thought that the jury would have enough evidence to come to a conclusion as to the cause of death. Wayman was present, but he (The Coroner) did not think he need be called.

The Foreman; He be treated as a witness I suppose?.

The Coroner; That is nothing to do with you. Mind your own business.

The Foreman; It is my business.

The Coroner; No it is not.

After this not very dignified passage of arms, the Coroner observed that the evidence was quite clear. These four little ones got down by the sea when the tide was coming in, and according to the evidence one of them appeared to fall in. The people who were about were very prompt in their efforts to effect a rescue and did all that could be done. He thought the Jury would have little difficulty in coming to a conclusion as to the cause of death, and that it was a case of "Accidentally drowned".

The Foreman said he thought they ought to acknowledge the admirable way in which Mrs. Crellin had acted and also the way in which the other witnesses performed their duty to those in danger. He also thought that the witnesses had given their evidence very clearly and straightforwardly.

The jury returned a verdict of "Accidentally drowned," and on the suggestion of the Foreman handed over their fees to the parents of the deceased child.

The Four Haverigg children involved were two sets of brothers, Thomas Gillbanks (deceased), Rodger Gillbanks , Harry Bird, and Michael Bird.

An example of a Bass caught on a Longline next to my size eleven welly.
(Kevin Alexander collection).

| five |

RESCUES AND NEAR MISSES

Millom Gazette, 7th July 1899.

BOAT CAPSIZED IN THE DUDDON.   NARROW ESCAPE OF FOUR MILLOM MEN.

On Sunday evening last, four young men hailing from Millom, had a narrow escape from drowning as the result of capsizing of a boat. It appears that on the evening in question the four young men whose names are Fred Riley, of the Furnace Yard, William Boyle, of Wellington Street, Gill, of Lord Street, and Christopher Vincent a son of Constable Vincent of Newton Street, obtained the loan of a boat belonging to Mr. Stephen Troughton, of the Peel Hotel, and moored near the Pier. In this craft which was none too seaworthy, it appears they set off for Foxfield. None of them were boating experts, and they had not gone far before they got out of their course. To make matters worse one or two of the men appeared to have been drinking, and this did not assist them in the management of the frail craft. When opposite Dunnerholme the boat from some reason or other upset and the occupants were thrown into the water. Fortunately, where the accident occurred the water was only shallow, and the men although almost up to the shoulders in the water were able to walk out. In this belated condition they proceeded to Askam, where Boyle, waxing eloquent upon the untoward turn of turn events had taken, was taken in custody by the Askam police. The others proceeded home by train, and appeared little worse for their waiting. At the Dalton Police Court on Monday morning Boyle was fined 10s, for being drunk and disorderly at Askam. The boat still lies in the vicinity of Dunnerholme.

A sailboat washed ashore at Dunnerholme.
(Courtesy of Norman Pascoe).

Millom Gazette, 6ᵀᴴ April 1900.

NARROW ESCAPES ON DUDDON SANDS.

Between one and two o'clock on Saturday morning an exciting incident occurred on Duddon Sands. It seems that two men had spent all Friday at Millom imbibing too freely, and having spent all their money they left Millom after closing time (eleven o'clock) for Barrow. They walked down to the shore near Millom Iron Works, and made their way across the sands, until they got into serious difficulties. The tide was rising rapidly, and the unlucky travellers speedily found themselves surrounded and in imminent danger of being drowned. Every moment their position became more precarious, and they called for help in vain. As yet the sand bank upon they stood was firm, but the cordon of water was drawing nearer and nearer, and they had almost given themselves up for lost when their cries were heard by Mr. Tom Constable, son of Mr. John Constable, fisherman of Askam. He quickly got a boat out, and rowed to the spot not a minute too soon, and after considerable difficulty he succeeded in rescuing the men. There was a strong current running at the time, and but for the timely arrival of Mr. Constable the two men would undoubtedly have been carried away. No sooner had he got the men into the boat than the sand bank upon which they were standing suddenly collapsed. One of the men was aged between 50 and 60 years of age, and he appeared to feel his position very keenly.

The West Cumberland News, 8th July 1893.

NARROW ESCAPE FROM DROWNING ON THE DUDDON SANDS.

On Thursday morning last Capt. H. Barlow-Massicks, the chairman of the Millom School Board and manager of the Millom Ironworks, together with his wife and coachman, had a narrow escape from drowning on the Duddon sands. It appears that an attempt was made by the party to cross the sands at low water with a pair of horses and four wheeler, and when crossing the stream the horses plunged into a hole completely immersing them. Mr. Barlow-Massicks was in possession of the reins, and he attempted to make for the other side of the stream when the carriage stuck and was entirely covered. Cushions, rugs, &c., were carried away by the stream, and Mrs. Barlow-Massicks was standing in the water up to the waist. The coachman essayed to get out and tried to lead the horses, but he could not bottom it. Fortunately some boys were cockling near by, and they ran for assistance. Mr. Wm Leece, belonging to the Hodbarrow pier at once came to their aid. He first of all swam across the stream, and then got hold of Mrs. Barlow-Massicks and conveyed her to a place of safety. Meanwhile the coachman had succeeded in liberating the horses, but none to soon, as one was on its side kicking and in a few minutes more it would have been drowned. The other animal, Fanny, a noted prize winner at many agricultural shows, made across to Askam, and when caught was almost exhausted. Beyond a ducking and the shock to the lady, the party were not much the worse.

Millom Gazette, 27th July, 1917.

DANGERS OF THE DUDDON.

Last week three Millom schoolboys, named Marr, Rigg, and Simpson, went to gather cockles on Duddon Sands, going out a considerable distance, in fact, so far that spectators on Millom Pier were unable to observe them. As the tide began to flow and fill the channels, one of the workmen on the pier expressed his anxiety about the three lads, but was told by his mates that they undoubtedly returned home. Mr. Procter was not, however, satisfied, and, independent of a severe wetting through having to wade through channels, found the three boys far out on the sands. He was only just in time, as they were beginning to be surrounded by the tide, and it was only with upmost difficulty, and by taking a roundabout road, that he was able to get them to a place of safety. One of the boys was nearly lost as it was. In the meantime the parents were anxiously awaiting the return of their children, who did not reach home until 10 o'clock at night, and then they were wet through, having to get through places where they were up to the neck in water.

Millom Gazette, 21ST August 1903.

BOAT RUN DOWN ON THE DUDDON AT ASKAM.

On Thursday evening a fishing boat, valued at £15, was run into and cut to pieces by the steam dredger, close to the Ironworks pier, belonging to the Millom and Askam Ironworks Company. The boat in question was the property of Mr. John Constable, fisherman, of Askam, and one young man had a very narrow escape of being killed.

Soulby's Ulverston Advertiser, 13th June 1912.

ACCIDENT AT DUDDON SANDS.

On Tuesday week, three men (Messers. J. Crank and J. Kirby, of Witbeck, and H. C. Kirby, of Ireleth), made an attempt to cross Duddon Sands to Ireleth with two horses, one in a conveyance and the other led with an halter. On entering the channel they suddenly made very deep water, and the horse, after swimming a short distance, sank, and was drowned. Fortunately, in the struggle of the horses, the conveyance was not overturned, and the three men were rescued from their perilous position by a boat from one of the vessels near, the horse that led was set at liberty and swam to shore.

Jim Alexander jr aboard the boat Susan, getting ready to trawl in the Duddon.
(Kevin Alexander collection).

| six |

IN TROUBLE WITH THE LAW

Fishing has always been a dangerous profession, a back breaking one with uncertainty attached to it. Back in the day a fisherman was not a wealthy person, they made enough to get by and that was about it. If they didn't catch, they didn't eat, they didn't have any money. They truly lived a hard life and so it was this need for survival that meant it was not unknown for some fishermen to come to blows and have bad blood between families. I have added two accounts regarding my own family fighting in this section. Some fishermen though took to stealing from others as a means of getting by or to just cause hardship to another fisherman because of a rivalry. However, the most common offence on the Duddon Sands would be that of taking a salmon without having a licence, only a few Duddon fishermen could afford a licence, and so the ones that did have they would be aggrieved at any one else taking the fish. It was the job of the water bailiffs to bring offenders to court as it still is today.

Millom Gazette, 11ᵀᴴ September 1903.

LOCAL FISHERY PROSECUTIONS AT MILLOM

On Saturday before Mr W. B. Walker (in the chair) and Mr. A. Watt.
The re-hearing took place in the prosecution case in which three Haverigg men were summoned by the Kent, Bela, etc., Fishery Board for fishing in their district for salmon with a certain device without a licence. The names of the defendants were Richard Edward Burt, William Burt and John Hodgson. At a previous sitting of the court the magistrates could not agree on the evidence given, and had ordered the case to be re-heard. Mr. Hart Jackson prosecuted , and asked that the case against Richard Edward Burt should be taken first, and he would stand by the decision.
This was agreed.
Mr. Hart Jackson in stating the case, said it was not necessary to prove that salmon had been caught, it was sufficient to prove that the defendant was fishing where salmon abounded. In this

particular case Edward Robinson, the Boards official had seen the defendants fishing at two o'clock in the morning in Haverigg Pool on June 22nd. Two draws were made by the defendants, and Robinson went to them and found they had a salmon net, for which they had no licence. A salmon net had an 8in. mesh.

Edward Robinson, beck watcher, was called and gave evidence as on the previous occasion. He saw the defendant admitted drawing in the Haverigg Pool from a boat. Defendant admitted he had no licence. Witness was sure he saw the defendant drawing in Haverigg Pool, which was a place where salmon lie.

In cross-examination witness held to his statement that the defendant was drawing in Haverigg pool. Defendant had a few fluke and codling in his boat, but no salmon.

Mr. Williams; You don't allege that he had any salmon? –

Witness; No.

Mr. Hart Jackson; We don't allege that.

A new witness was called, named Saml. Sage, who said he was a licenced salmon fisher. On June 22nd he saw the defendant and others in a boat between twelve o'clock and two o'clock in the morning. They were drawing from Haverigg Pool to the Mussel Scar.

Cross-examined; Witness saw defendant drawing perhaps a dozen times in Haverigg Pool, where it empties itself into the channel. He could see him distinctly, being only eight yards away from witness at one time. About a year ago he had a "row" with defendant but he denied that he had said he would "have it in for Burt."

Mr. Hart Jackson; You have to pay £5 for your licence to catch salmon, and you do not like to see others fishing without a licence? – No, Sir.

Ernest Sage, brother of the last witness gave evidence as to seeing the defendant in Haverigg Pool on that date.

Cross-examined; You were not fishing? – No.

How was that? – it was close time.

Close time? – Yes.

The Magistrates' Clerk; Your men were fishing Mr Williams (laughter).

Mr. Hart Jackson; He can have a double summons if he likes (laughter).

Mr. Watt; It was the weekly close time you mean? –

Witness; Yes.

Mr. Williams said the defence was that his client did not fish in Haverigg Pool, Haverigg Pool mouth, or anywhere in the Kent, Bela, etc., district. Had they been drawing for salmon they would of caught at least some salmon in the drawing. The defendant Burt was called and in his evidence said he was employed on the sea wall, and also did some fishing. On June 22nd he and his brother were out fishing with 7in. mesh net at any time.

Cross-examined; Haverigg Pool was two miles from Haverigg Point, and Duddon Bar three miles further out.

Mr. Hart Jackson; Haverigg Pool is only three-quarters of a mile from Haverigg Point. Here is the plan (produced).

Defendant, in further cross-examination, said Duddon Bar was seven miles out, on that morning he came up with the tide and covered 2 ½ miles in a quarter of an hour.

Mr. Hart Jackson; Rowing?

Defendant; Yes, I can row.

Mr. Hart Jackson; I thought you must have had a steam engine. (laughter).

Wm. Henry Burt was called next. He said they only drew on Duddon Bar, and did not fish in Haverigg Pool at all.

In cross-examination, witness said he did not think they could catch salmon with a fluke net. It was seven miles to Duddon Bar, and they came back on the flood tide, and did the seven miles in about an hour. The tide was making strong.

The question arose as to when it was it was high water, and Mr. Hart Jackson called Capt. Joseph Jones who said he was the Pier and Berthing Master at the Port of Barrow. He produced the tide book, showing that on the evening of June 21st, it was high water at Barrow at 8.20 and on the morning of the 22nd at 8.32. The Millom tides were 12 minutes later. It would be dead low water at Haverigg about 2.46 in the morning and about 2.14 on Duddon Bar, in the first hour it would run at two knots on the flood; It never reached a velocity of eight knots. It was a very clear night.

Cross-examined; The tide never, in his experience ran more than 4 ½ knots. That was 14 years ago.

John Nelson Hodgson, of Haverigg, said that on this day the Burt's gave him sail down from under Duddon Bar. There was no fishing whilst he was with them.

Cross-examined; He did not know Haverigg Point. He left Haverigg at nearly one o'clock in the morning and did not know at what time he got under Duddon Bar. He was in Burt's boat about half an hour but he did not know.

Mr. Hart Jackson remarked that this man did not appear to know anything.

The Bench considered the case proved and Burt was fined £5 including costs.

The cases against William Burt and John Hodgson who were in the boat along with defendant Richard Edward Burt, were next taken; and the two defendants were let off on payment of costs.

Thomas Hoskin and Solomon Haddeth were summoned for fishing for salmon without a licence, and were fined 10s. including costs.

Soulby's Ulverston Advertiser and General Intelligencer,
25TH October 1906.

TROUBLE AT ASKAM. RIVAL COCKLERS DISAGREE. POLICE COURT SEQUEL.

The sequel of a cocklers' row was heard at the Ulverston Police Court on Thursday before Col. Baldwin and other magistrates.

Rebecca Alexander lodged a charge of assault against Mary Ann Turner, and the husband of the latter was charged on a cross-summons with assaulting Mrs. Alexander. Mr. F. W. Poole appeared for the Turners, and Mr. R. B. Jackson for Mrs Alexander, all being from Askam.

Mrs, Turner stated that on the 22nd of August last she was on the Askam sands along with her husband gathering cockles, when they saw Mrs. Alexander approaching. There had been some former disputes about cockling, and, thinking there was going to be some bother, they set off towards home. Mrs. Alexander followed, and having thrown a stone at her, picked up a large piece of slag. Her husband (Turner) interfered, and gave Mrs. Alexander a push, when she fell upon her knees. When she got up she continued the stone throwing, and complainant was struck upon the arm and head.

Complainant's husband corroborated, and denied that he had struck Mrs. Alexander in the face, and knelt on her.

Mrs. Tinning, of Sharp-street, Askam, spoke to seeing Mrs. Alexander the day after the alleged assault. At that time there were no marks upon her.

On the other side, Mrs. Alexander alleged that the row was begun by the Turners. She (witness) was on the sands cockling along with her daughter and two little sons, when they had some words with the Turners, which ended in Turner striking her twice in the face, which was discoloured. She fell down, and she remembered no more. If there was any stone-throwing, it was done by boys after Turner's attack upon her.

Mr. Alexander stated that when he appeared on the scene he saw Turner striking her in the face, and when she fell he knelt upon her and hit her about the head with a cockle cran.

A son of the former witness gave corroborative evidence.

Dr. Cook spoke to attending Mrs. Alexander on the Monday after the accident. Her cheek bone was discoloured.

Henry Turner was fined 20s. and costs for assaulting Mrs. Alexander, and the advocates fee was allowed. The charge preferred by Mrs. Turner against Mrs. Alexander was dismissed.

Soulby's Ulverston Advertiser, 9TH July 1857.

HEARTLESS ROBBERY.

Two poor industrious fishermen named John Todd and John Gillbanks, of Sandside, Kirkby Ireleth, have for some time had cause to suspect that their nets on Duddon Sands were plundered. This suspicion was, on Sunday morning last, changed into certainty by the discovery of the thieves. We understand that a compromise took place, the fellows paying the value of the fish they had taken. To rob the poor fisherman, whose occupation is so toilsome and so dangerous, of the fruit of his labour is about as heartless a robbery as can be committed.

A brilliant and rare photo of Bird's Cottage with Father Bird's big boat out front.
(Courtesy of Margaret Edmondson).

A view towards Sandscale point, with Bird's Cottage shed and boat in the foreground.
(From the Gaythorpe Collection. Copyright of Cumbria Archives).

Barrow Herald, 22ND December 1866.

ROBBING A BOAT ON DUDDON SANDS.

James and John Bird, brothers, and sons of R. Bird, fisherman, Roanhead, Duddon, were charged by Mr. B. D. Healey, of this town, with stealing from his boat, on the 7th of September last, 11 blocks, one sail, and a quantity of rope.

Mr. Healey, deposed; I am a clerk in the employ of Barrow Hematite Steel Company. I had a boat called the " Valencia," and left her stranded on Duddon Sands, on the 3rd of September last, after having a voyage to the Isle of Man. When I last saw her she was complete in all her rigging, &c., I missed the articles of about the 8th of the same month. I was informed of what was missing on the 6th, which was transmitted by telegraph from Furness Abbey, saying that the "vessel was stripped." The ropes and sails produced are mine. I can swear to them both.

By Mr. Cooper; I have not seen them since the time they were stolen until Saturday last, when I saw them in a boat at the bottom of Mr. Gradwell's Pier. I was told by William Thompson that he had seen some of my stolen property in the boat named.

William Thompson stated; I am a stonemason by trade, but at the moment I am trouling (Trawling) in Barrow Channel. I had just come from onboard a vessel with a companion, and thought we would go and look at a boat that was getting repaired at the jetty end of Mr. Gradwell's pier. There was a lot of rope and a sail on board in a bag. I thought they were very much like the those stolen from Mr. Healey's boat. I went for Mr. Healey, and told him what I had seen. Sergeant Cross asked if I could swear to the rope, but I told him that I could not as it was a bad thing to swear to. I left Mr. Healey's boat, complete in all rigging and running gear, on the 3rd of September. I was told that the boat belonged to Mr Bird, of Roanhead, in which I found the articles; she was getting made into a fishing boat. I saw the boat all night on the 6th of September, and on the 7th I found 11 blocks, one jib, one foresail, ropes and rigging were all gone.

John Christopherson said; I am a sail-maker, in the employ of T. Ashburner and co., of Barrow. I can swear to the sail produced as being one I assisted to make July last, it has since been cut in different places and fresh pieces put in.

Mr. Henry Stuart, rope manufacturer, said; I cannot positively swear that I made the rope produced, but at the same time I firmly believe that it was made by me for Mr. Healey's boat. It is a peculiar make. I never made a rope like it for anyone else. It corresponds with the entry in my books for the rope I made Mr. Healey.

Sergeant Cross, deposed; On Saturday last, from information received, I went to Mr. Gradwell's yard. I found the ropes and sails produced in a boat which the prisoner, James Bird, said belonged to him. Neither of the prisoners were on board when I took possession of the articles. I asked him if he had a boat getting repaired at Mr. Gradwell's yard, and he replied that he had. I said how do you account for those ropes and rigging being on board? – "my father bought them." Mr. Healey, I said, had identified them as stolen from his boat in September last. He answered, "Oh, my brother John found them on the sands." We went up to his brother who replied, "no, I did not find them," but soon after admitted that he found the rope on the sands.

James Bird, the elder of the two lads, said the sail was made at Morecambe for his fathers big boat. When I got to the police station I asked James if those were the ropes and sails he left on the boat, to which he replied in the affirmative.

Mr. Healey, cross-examined by Mr. Graham; The value of the stolen property would be about £12.

P.C. Issacs said; I apprehended John Bird this morning as he was coming from Ireleth, when he said that he, his brother, and another lad had found the ropes on the sands about six weeks ago.

The prisoners on being asked if they had anything to say, or any questions to ask, replied that they had not.

They were both committed to stand their trial at the next quarter sessions.

This next story, I can add some personal insight as it regards my family directly. The story relates to a fight that occurred between my family and that of the Birbeck's. The Birbeck's, on the morning of the fight, had put their stake net close to the Alexander net to cause trouble. Both families had already exchanged heated conversations regarding fishing several times before. On the evening of the fight, James and Sam Alexander were tending to their net when William, Henry and James Birbeck walked past them towards their net further on. As they passed, apparently Henry Birbeck under the influence of alcohol, threatened them. The Birbeck's tended their net and came past again and attacked. A crowd of between 30 and 40 people seemed to have followed the Birbeck's almost like they had been told a fight would occur.

Barrow News, 30th May 1931.

ASKAM MEN COMMITTED FOR TRIAL.

WITNESSES' STORY OF AFFAIR ON DUDDON SANDS.

CHARGES AGAINST TWO OF THE MEN DISSMISSED.

THREE DAYS' HEARING OF THE CASE AT ULVERSTON.

After a hearing that has occupied the best part of three days, the case against a number of Askam fishermen, charged with being concerned in an affray on Duddon Sands, as a result of which several of them were severely injured, on the evening of April 23rd, was concluded at Ulverston Magistrates' Court on Tuesday. In the result five of the Askam men have been committed for trial at the next Lancaster Assizes, and released on bail.

Originally seven men were charged. One of these was so severely injured that he had to remain in hospital for about a fortnight, the hearing of the charges being adjourned in consequence. The following have been committed for trial:-

William Alexander, senr. (60), William Alexander, junr. (39), James Alexander, (17), and Samuel Alexander (21), all charged with wounding Samuel Birbeck with intent to do him grievous bodily harm.

Henry Birbeck (35), charged with wounding William Alexander, senr, and Samuel Alexander with intent to do them grievous bodily harm. Charges brought against James Birbeck (30) and William Birbeck (22) in connection with the affair were dismissed. The men committed for trial were allowed bail in the sum of £25 each.

At the hearing of the charges, which commenced on Thursday week and continued on Saturday and Tuesday, the Birbecks were defended by Mr. Stanley Fisher and the Alexanders by Mr. F. W. Poole. The magistrates on the bench were Ald. S. Taylor (in the chair). Mr. J. Walker, Mr. J. H. Ellwood, and Mr. D. Lawn.

The proceedings at the opening of the case on Thursday week were fully reported in last week's issue of the "News." When the hearing was continued on Saturday, the cross-examination of James Alexander (17) was resumed by Mr. Fisher.

Mr. Fisher; You Spoke to Stevenson. Was it before the Birbecks returned ? Was it about that time your father shouted to you? -

Witness; Yes.

Was the net at which you were working about the spot of no. 5 pit ? – No, nearer the locks(lots).

Do you remember what time it was when you went to your net ? – About half-past seven. When I left home.

Would it take about a quarter of an hour to the net ?- Yes.

You had been working at your net about an hour before the Birbecks arrived?- No, about half an hour.

When they left to your net was it still light ? – It would be closing in dusk.

Had they to go another 300 yards ? – Yes.

Could you see them at their net ? – Yes.

Was your Teddy at your net ? – No.

WOMAN'S EVIDENCE.

The next witness was Jane Alexander, a single woman, residing at 34, Furnace Place, Askam, who said that between 8.30 and 9 o'clock, when she went down on to the Askam foreshore in consequence of what she had been told, she there saw a crowd of men, which included the three accused, surrounding her brother, Samuel, who was lying on the ground. Her brothers, James and William, were also there. She also saw her father, who was bleeding from the ear, and his face was covered with blood. Immediately her brother Samuel got up from the ground, and she saw he was bleeding from the face. William Birbeck had a net stake in his hand (similar to the one produced). The four Birbecks were chasing her brothers James and William. Her brother William had called to her to go for the police.

Cross-examined by Mr. Fisher, the witness said it was practically dark when she got on to the shore.

It was so dark that you could not see more than a few yards in front of you ? – No, sir; not when I first got on to the shore.

Was John Bodley there also? – Not then.

He was actually on the shore when you got back the second time ? – Yes.

Did you say, "If it had not been for my father there would have been none of this" ? – No, sir.

Did Bodley ask you who the men were on the other side of the channel ? – No.

Did you hear him call across "where's Birbeck" ? – No.

Did you hear your brother William shout " You know as much as I b_ well do" ? – No.

WENT FOR THE POLICE.

In reply to further questions witness said, the fight had started before she went for the police. Her brother Samuel was on the ground, and her father had just got up and was going home.

Where was your brother Teddy ? – He was not there, he was ill in bed. He got up and went on the shore afterwards to meet my brother, after the fight was over.

Edward Alexander was the next witness called. He said he was a labourer on the L.M and S. Railway Engineering Department, residing at 34, Furnace Place, Askam. About 8.30 p.m. on the date in question he was in bed suffering from influenza. In consequence of what his mother told him he struggled out of bed and went down to the beach, where he saw his brother Sam coming off the shore. Blood was falling from his head on to his clothes down the front. He did not see any of his other brothers or his father; neither did he see any of the Birbecks.

It would be turned 9 o'clock when he reached the place where he met his brother Samuel. It was dark.

In reply Mr. Fisher, witness said he did not see his sister Jane on the shore. Nor his brother William. He saw John Bodley, who was quite near to him. Did you pick up a stake and strike Birbeck ? – No.

And did Henry Birbeck ward off the blow and strike you with his fist and knock you on the sand ? – No.

How long had you been in bed with the flu ? – Since 3 o'clock the day before.

Wm. Hewitson, iron-ore miner, residing at 94 Steel-Street, Askam, said that about 10 o'clock on Saturday, April 25th , he was shown the spade produced by P.C. Parkinson and identified it as his property, and the one he had lent to either Henry or William Birbeck about a month previously.

William Maxwell Stevenson, an unemployed labourer residing at 123, Sharp-Street, Askam, when his attention was drawn to Samuel Birbeck, whom he recognised by his voice. He could see he was fighting with two or three more, and he heard the blows, stakes being used. A few minutes afterwards he heard William Alexander shouting "Come on you three." Witness was shrimping, and walked down the Channel to the nets. He also saw James, and two others assembled on the shore before he left. Mr. Fisher cross-examined the witness at some length.

IN THE DUSK.

Joseph Bodley, a labourer, living at 153, Sharp-Street, Askam, said that shortly after 9 o'clock on Thursday, April 23rd, in consequence of what his sister-in-law told him, he went down to the shore, just on the dry-water channel. When he got there he saw Jane Alexander with a net stake, and William Alexander, junr. He also saw about four or five forms in the dusk.

In reply to Mr. Fisher witness said he did not see any blows struck. He saw Samuel Birbeck, who came past where he was standing on the dry-water channel. Witness noticed he could scarcely walk and was staggering forward, and his clothes seemed to be wet.

John Bodley, of 90, Steel-Street, Askam, said that about 8.30 he was on the shore at Askam and met Samuel Birbeck. After reaching home and hearing of the disturbance, he returned to the shore about a quarter to nine. He met Jane Alexander and stopped there with her. He also saw William Alexander, junr., and his brother Edward, but nothing of the Birbecks.

In reply to Mr. Fisher, witness said he asked Jane Alexander what had been going on, and she said "If it hadn't been for my father there would have been none of it." He asked her who was on the other side, and she made no reply. He could not recognise the figures as it was too dark, although they were only ten yards away. He shouted across the channel, "Where's Henry Birbeck ?" and recognised William Alexander's voice shouting back. "You'll know as much as I do." He then went across the channel and saw both William and Edward Alexander.

Mr. Fisher; Edward Alexander has sworn in the box that he was not across the channel on that particular evening, what have you got to say to that ?

Witness; I say he was.

How long were the police after you in getting to the shore ? – Ten minutes.

How many would there be in the crowd ? – About 30 or 40.

CUTS OVER HEAD.

P.C. Parkinson, stationed at Askam, said at 9 p.m. on Thursday, April 23rd. He was in company of Sergt. Law, and in consequence of what he was told went on to the shore at Askam, and saw a crowd of people coming from the shore. Near the water's edge he saw Samuel Alexander, who was bleeding freely from the bridge of the nose and two cuts over the left eyebrow. Witness took him to Askam Police Station and rendered him first aid. Shortly afterwards William Alexander, senr., came to Askam Police Station. Samuel(William senr.) Alexander's left ear was almost severed from his head and he was bleeding profusely. About 10.30 p.m. the accused Henry Birbeck , came into the police station, accompanied by his brother Samuel. Samuel was in a fainting condition and had a deep scalp wound.

In consequence of a statement made by William Alexander, senr., he took Henry Birbeck into custody and charged him with unlawfully and maliciously wounding William Alexander and also with wounding Samuel Alexander by striking them with a spade. He replied " How can I strike a man when I was on the ground with a man holding a double-barrelled sporting gun at me. That was William Alexander, the old fellow's son."

The constable later visited Birbeck's house and took possession of the spade (produced), which he found in the back yard. It was very wet and covered in wet sand. The following day at 3.30 p.m. he interviewed James Birbeck, of Steel-street, Askam. After cautioning him he said he was making inquiries respecting an affray on the shore, the previous night. He also told him he would be detained pending inquiries. At 1.15 p.m. the same date he took possession of the gun (produced) which was handed him by the wife of William Alexander, junr., and later that day cautioned and charged the three accused together. Henry Birbeck replied. " Carry on," William Birbeck made no reply, and James Birbeck replied. "We hadn't a _ spade; we are two(too) _ English to have one." Whilst the men were in custody William Birbeck said he wished to make a statement. James Birbeck also wished to make a statement.

The written record of these two statements were produced in court and read. In reply to Mr. Fisher, witness said he asked Mrs. William Alexander if she had a gun and she said she had not one in the house. She later handed the constable the gun (produced) which was hanging on the wall.

CUTS ON THE FACE.

Sergeant Law, stationed at Askam, said that when he reached the shore he saw Samuel Alexander standing by the water's edge. He had a deep cut on his nose and two over his left eyebrow. G=He asked Henry Birbeck if the spade was his and he replied, "I would rather not say." Witness then asked him, "Did you not tell me that the spade was Alexander's last night ? " Birbeck replied, "I am not going to say anything about it until I see which way this thing is going."

P.C. Parkinson, recalled, gave evidence as to serving copies of the statements (made by the accused) on each of the other Birbecks.

A previous witness John Bodley, was also recalled and questioned by Mr. Fisher. This closed the case for the prosecution against Henry Birbeck.

Mr. Fisher, for the defence, submitted that not sufficient evidence had been presented to support the charges against James Birbeck.

The magistrates retired for consultation. On their return, the chairman said the bench proposed to listen to what the defence had to say with regard to James and William Birbeck, as they were of the opinion their cases were those of common assault , and they would not proceed with more serious charges in the case of those two.

ONE MAN FOR TRAIL.

The chairman, addressing Henry Birbeck, the first of the accused, said; You are charged with wounding Wm. Alexander with intent to do him grievous bodily harm, and similarly charged in respect to Samuel Alexander. Have you anything to say.

Henry Birbeck; No, sir.

Mr. Fisher intimated that the accused would reserve his defence.

Henry Birbeck was then committed for trail at the next Lancaster Assizes. He was allowed bail in the sum of £25. An application by Mr. Fisher for legal aid certificate was granted.

Mr. Fisher said it was the contention of the defence in the two cases of common assault that the whole of the trouble arose out of jealousy on the part of the Alexander family, all of whom did a certain amount of fishing, and the defendant resented anyone coming to certain places on the foreshore and setting nets. He suggested that the bench "could not possibly have heard more contradictory evidence."

THROWN INTO THE CHANNEL.

Samuel Birbeck, the first witness called for the defence, said he had no interest in fishing. On the evening in question he set off to go along the shore, leaving the house at 8.40 p.m. He kept to the shore, and when he got to the bridge he met Jack Bodley and Wm. Askew. He said he had walked some distance when five Alexanders "ran out at him," knocking him to the ground, and carrying him a distance of 50 yards and throwing him into the channel.

James Birbeck said he went to his net in company with his brother William. They set off for home when Alexander, senr., shouted, "Come on lads; let the __ have it now; we have got them all here." There was a fight afterwards. He dragged his brother Sam away unconscious, to save him from any more blows. He heard his brother shout, "Is that you Harry?." When he got to his brother Samuel he took hold of him. At no time had he a stick, nor did he strike Samuel Alexander. He did not see his brother William strike, his whole attention being taken up with his brother Samuel.

Wm. Askew, of Queen-street, Askam, said he visited the shore about 8.30 p.m. The first person he saw was Jane Alexander. James Birbeck remained with his brother. He did not see James Birbeck or William Birbeck strike Samuel Alexander.

In reply to the chairman, he said he did not see any blows struck.

Wm. Birbeck said he was carrying a spade. He saw the Alexanders, and said they were knocking his brother with stakes. Four or five surrounded him. The stake belonged to Edward Alexander.

Mr. Fisher; Did you knowingly strike Samuel Alexander? – No, sir.

Did you use any more force than was necessary to protect yourself? - No.

Did you see your brother James? – Not at all.

CASES DISMISSED.

The bench hereupon dismissed the cases against James Birbeck and William Birbeck.

Supt. Crapper then preceded with the prosecution of William Alexander senior, William Alexander junior, James Alexander and Samuel Alexander. Charged with wounding and assaulting Samuel Birbeck. The Supt. Said that the facts were largely as stated in opening the first case.

Samuel Birbeck, a general labourer, residing at 113, Steel-Street, Askam, said he recalled a day last July when gathering winkles on the shore at Askam. He heard one of the Alexander's say to his brother Henry, "I will bring the gun and blow your __ brains out." His brother told William Alexander, junior, not to be so silly as he would fight him a fair fight any time. No further quarrel occurred until April 23rd, this year. He was walking along the beach and saw the four Alexanders and another called Bob. He noticed that William Alexander, junior, had a gun under his right arm, and the other four had fish net-stakes. They "Set about him" right away.

"LET HIM DROWN."

He heard one of them say , "Take him to the channel; throw him in and let him drown." The second time he saw the Alexanders all three had stakes and all struck him with them. He later found himself at 84, Steel-Street, Askam. His injuries, he said included a cut over the head 2 ½ inches long. He was also bruised about the body and arms. After attention by the ambulance men, he was attended by Dr. Southern.

Cross-examined by Mr. Poole, the witness said there was "nothing unusual" going on the shore.

Mr. Poole; Why did you send Hewitson for the Police?

Witness; Because William Alexander shouted "Come on, chaps, get to the other __."

You were assaulted by five men. Nearly drowned, and yet you went to assist your brothers? – No.

Could you see anything on the shore? – I saw a crowd.

When you got back on the second occasion, a crowd had assembled? -Yes.

Witness, in further cross-examination, denied that he was attracted to the shore by hearing voices, and went armed with a stick with a knob on it, and that he aimed a blow at the younger Alexander, who took the stick off him.

STAKING STAKES.

Henry Birbeck, of 84, Steel-street, Askam, said he remembered about 8 a.m. on Thursday morning he went to his brother James's net. One of the Alexanders (James) came out to their net to do fishing. When he passed him and he put some stakes in, James Alexander went home. Wm. Alexander, senior, came down and said, "What do you mean by putting the stakes in front of our Sam's net?" witness replied "We have equally as much right to put those stakes there." Alexander said to witness "I think you are asking for trouble." Witness asked, "Who with?" and he replied, " My son, William, I'll bring him to you, and he'll knock hell out of you." Witness said, "Go and bring him; we'll see if he'll knock hell out of me." When he was going away he said "You'll see!".

About 8.30 the same evening witness went to the nets with his two brothers, William and James, and took the fish out of the nets. His brothers were cleaning the arm of the net while he was sanding the corner of the net. After he set off for home they passed three men – Edward and Harry Alexander and another. About 30 or 40 yards further on, Wm. Alexander, sen., came running across the bank, shouting to his sons. "Come on, here they are!". One of Alexander's sons shouted to his father, telling him to get himself off home. They saw someone making towards them, heard someone shout, "Harry! Harry!". Witness ran to his brother's assistance and there were Alexanders – William, sen., William, jun., Edward, James, Samuel and Harry – all standing over his brother "braying" him with net stakes.

IN THE MALEE.

His brothers, James and William were following on behind, and as soon as witness got up Edward Alexander ran at him with a net stake. He was delivering his blow when witness guarded the blow off with his left hand and struck him in the jaw with his right fist. He was bruised on the arm between the wrist and the elbow by the blow.

"William Alexander (continued witness), rushed at me with a gun, and I made a grab and got the gun by the barrel. Whilst I was struggling with him with the gun, old Alexander came and hit me at the back of my head with a net stake. I got up and ran perhaps 20 yards to where my brother William had left his spade. I went back with the spade and made for the man with the gun, and drove him across the dead water channel. A crowd gathered and he said, "Come on Harry, I've been waiting for you." He was retreating. When the crowd said the police were coming Samuel Alexander was charging him with a net stake, and he was guarding him off, and jabbed him with the spade. "Old William, likely, got in the road, same as the rest." Later witness went for the police, with his brother Samuel.

Mr. Poole (cross-examining); Your object in going to the police station to make a voluntary statement was to mislead the police? – No, sir.

You didn't say anything to the police about jabbing anyone with a spade then? – No, I didn't say anything about the spade.

You say, in in the voluntary statement, that you were knocked off your feet and young Will Alexander stood over you with a double-barrelled sporting gun? – Yes.

Yet in the box to-day you could not say definitely that it was a double-barrelled gun? – I felt it was by the barrel.

ATTACK OR DEFENCE?

You got the spade and made for the man with the gun. You do admit you attacked with the spade? – I did not attack, I defended myself.

Dr. Southern said that on being called to Askam Police Station he found Samuel Birbeck suffering from a deep cut on the scalp, 2 ½ inches long. Witness stitched the wound. He also found the man to be suffering from bruises on his scalp and weals on the body, shock, and loss of blood, and he advised his removal to hospital, but he refused to go.

James Birbeck, a labourer, residing at 84, Steel-Street, Askam, said he was on the shore with his brothers, William and Henry, attending to the nets. He had just finished and was about to return home when he heard the Alexander, sen., shout, "Come on lads, give the __s it while we have got them 'em together." Before that one of the Alexanders shouted to his father, "Get yourself to__ out of it," and the elder Alexander said, "Come on, while we've got 'em here!" A form was coming towards him in the dusk, and he recognised the voice of his brother, Samuel. He went to his assistance and while he was attending to him, they attacked Henry and William. He also heard William Alexander, junr., say to his brother, Henry, " I have been waiting a long while for you, Harry, I'll blow your __ brains out as soon as you get in reach." He heard women in the crowd say to William Alexander, " For Gods sake think of your wife and kids."

The witness was cross-examined by Mr. Poole, respecting discrepancies in his voluntary statement and his evidence given in court.

"FINISH THEM OFF!"

William Birbeck gave evidence that at 8.30 on the evening of the 23rd he and his brothers went to the shore. They did not see any of the Alexanders until they were coming home, when they saw three of them. He saw his brother Samuel making towards him. As he approached he called out, "Make this way, lads; they are waiting for you in this hollow," and Wm. Alexander was carrying a gun and witness heard somebody shout, "For God's sake don't do it! think about your wife and kids!" He had dropped the spade some yards back.

Mr. Poole; How did your brother get the spade again? – My brother went back for the spade to shield himself in self-defence. He got it and entered into affray again with the result that he jabbed and injured two of the Alexanders? – No, I didn't see that.

How far was your brother Samuel from you? – From 30 and 40 yards on the right-hand side.

He was nearer to you than Alexander, sen.? – Yes.

How many were there with Alexander, sen.? – Four.

The four you could see immediately attacked your brother Samuel, and you and your other brother went to his assistance? – yes.

And they were still beating him? – Yes.

At 6.30 p.m. the Court adjourned till Tuesday.

At the resumption of the hearing on Tuesday, William Askew, an iron ore miner, residing at 139, Steel-street, Askam, was the first witness called. He stated that at 9 p.m. on April 23rd he was on the shore and there he saw Samuel Birbeck bleeding from the head, which was running down each side of the cheek. His clothing appeared to be very wet. He also saw James, Ted, and William Alexander, jun. He saw Samuel Birbeck come down and cross the channel. William Alexander, jun, came on the scene, and, making a motion to his pocket, warned them to stand back, saying to the crowd, "If you come over here I'll blow your brains out." He saw fighting going on, but he could not tell who the men were, as he was too far away. He saw a figure on the floor on his hands and knees and made across to him, and when he got there found it was Samuel Birbeck.

Mr. Poole; In consequence of what you were told, you went down to the shore and saw Samuel Birbeck come down after two or three minutes and cross the channel. Did you notice whether he was carrying anything? -No, sir.

At that time he was not bleeding from the head? – No.

And William Alexander was then at least 10 yards away from you? – Yes.

Edward was with William at this time and a crowd was gathering? – Yes.

"TROUBLE GOING ON."

And the trouble was going on, on the sands, about 150 yards away? – Yes.

And Samuel Birbeck made for where the trouble was going on? – Yes.

William Alexander had nothing in his hand to carry out his threat of shooting? – Not that I could see.

Sergeant Law, stationed at Askam, said that at 9.30p.m. on Thursday, April 23rd in consequence of what he was told, he went on to the shore at Askam, in company with P.C. Parkinson, and later saw Samuel Birbeck at the Police Station. The latter then had a wound on the top of his head about 2 ½ inches long. At 11.30 the following day he saw the accused, James Alexander, in Furnace-Place, Askam. He cautioned him and told him he was making inquiries regarding the affray on the shore at Askam the previous day, and that he would be detained pending inquiries. He took him to the Police Station. At 6.30 p.m. the same day he saw William Alexander, junr., in company with Det. Constable Rothwell. He cautioned him and told him he was making inquiries regarding the affray on the shore at Askam the previous day and that he would be detained pending inquiries.

HIT WITH SPADE.

Det.-Con. Jas. Smith Rothwell said that at 1 p.m on April 24th he interviewed William Alexander, sen. He cautioned him, and told him he was a detective from Ulverston making inquiries into the Askam affray. He made a statement, which witness took down in his pocket-book. This was now read in court.

This contained the following :-

" Between 8.30 and 9 p.m. on April 23rd, I went towards a group of my sons, Jim and Sam, and the Birbecks, who were 'rowing' on the shore. The Birbecks and mates around our Sam beating him. I ran off to call the police.

"IF I HAD A GUN –"

"As I was running away Harry Birbeck hit me four times on the head with a spade, and made a cut which nearly took my left ear off. There has been trouble for months over the fishing between the two families of us. I have no gun, but if I had a gun I would shoot the lot of the Birbecks if I had plenty of shot. But I was attacked before I struck a blow. I only had a walking stick with me"

At 1.20p.m. the same day, witness again saw William Alexander, senior, at this moment he cautioned him, and told him he would be detained pending inquiries. Witness was present later that day when accused was charged with the offence by P.C. Parkinson. At 6.20 the same day in company with Sergt. Law, he saw William Alexander, junior, he was also present later the same day, when the latter was cautioned and charged by P.C. Parkinson.

Mr. Poole; Where was his gun found? – William Alexander, juniors, house, hanging on the wall.

It was not a likely weapon for a man to take to a scrap, is it? – No.

P.C. Parkinson, stationed at Askam related the events that occurred on April 23rd on the shore. He said that Samuel Alexander was standing by himself near the water's edge. He had a deep cut on the bridge of his nose, and two deep cuts on the left eyebrow. Witness later dressed these injuries at the police station. Shortly afterwards, the accused, Wm. Alexander, senr., came to the police station with his ear almost severed from his head.

About 11.30 p.m. the same day Henry Birbeck and his brother Samuel came to the police station, the latter being in a fainting condition. His injuries had to be dressed, and witness later saw a cut on his head. It was a deep scalp wound across the top. Both his arms were also bruised. On the following day he cautioned the three accused, Wm. Alexander, senr., Wm. Alexander, junr., and Jas. Alexander. Charging them together that they did at about 8.30 p.m. on Thursday the 23rd April, 1931, unlawfully and maliciously cut and wound Samuel Birbeck by striking him on the head with a sharpened wooden fish-net stakes on the shore at Askam.

Wm. Alexander, senr., Replied " I can't be charged, I was attacked."

Wm. Alexander, junr., Replied "We will reserve all evidence until the court. There is only one thing I will say, and that is it will be very difficult for the Birbecks to get any witnesses except for the police."

Jas. Alexander made no reply.

"I WAS ATTACKED."

At 3.15 p.m. on May 18 he apprehended accused, Samuel Alexander, on a warrant at his home. He cautioned him and read the warrant to him and he replied; "There is only one fault in it, that's all."

Samuel Birbeck; "I never touched him."

The same day he served copies of the statements made by Henry and James Birbeck on each of the accused.

William Alexander, senr., replied, " I should not be in it, I was attacked."

William Alexander, junr., James and Samuel Alexander made no reply.

Samuel Birbeck, Henry Birbeck, James Birbeck and William Birbeck were here called whilst the statements he had made was read over to him by the magistrates' clerk.

P.C. Parkinson, in answer to Mr. Poole, said he had not been able to ascertain that any of the Alexanders had had a gun during the past two years, with the exception of the rifle produced.

THE DEFENCE.

Mr. F. W. Poole, for the defence, said some of the evidence had been proved to be absolutely false. That of the witness Askew, an entirely independent witness, was contradictory to that of Birbecks'. He submitted that there was no case on which the accused could be committed for trail.

The bench retired for consultation, and on their return the Chairman, addressing Mr. Poole, said they had decided to over-rule his submission.

The accused were then formally charged by the Clerk, with "wounding Samuel Birbeck with intent to do him harm on the 23rd April," and Mr. Poole proceeded to call evidence.

"LET ME BE AT HIM."

Samuel Alexander, a fisherman , of 34, Furnace-Place, Askam, said he was fishing at his nets on the evening of April 23rd. He and his brother, James, went down to the nets about 7.30, and Henry, William and James Birbeck came to them whilst they were there. Henry Birbeck said, "Let me be at him; I will cut him in two and throw him in the channel." He was carrying a spade at the time, and was the worse for drink and his two brothers, James and William, tried to get him away, and eventually they got him away, and they went down to their own net, 200 yards further away. Witness and his brother were still at their own net when the Birbecks came back again, passing within 300 yards. At that time his brothers, Henry and James, were with him. He left his brother Edward in bed, and he never came to the net. His father was shouting to them to "come off," and the Birbecks were 30 yards away from his father. As soon as he (witness) got near, Henry Birbeck hit him with the spade. At that time he saw nothing of Samuel Birbeck. He denied that he and his father and brothers beat Samuel Birbeck.

James Alexander was also called.

William Alexander, junr., denied that any member of his family had a gun of any description during that evening. When he met Samuel Birbeck the man carrying a net stake and was making in the direction of the nets.

Further questioned by Mr. Poole as to what happened on that occasion, witness said; " I said to him, 'where are you going Sam? Don't go across there to make any bother, Sam; keep yourself back'." Birbeck then struck at witness with a spar and he warded the blow and took the stick from him, pushing him in the face. He fell to the ground. Witness stayed by the edge of the dead-water channel, and a crowd began to collect shortly afterwards. They all came from the Steel-street side, and they also began to collect against the dead-water channel. He never saw his brother Edward. Witness did not see either Henry Birbeck or his (witness's) father. He was chased back across the dead-water channel by William and James Birbeck. He denied that he joined his father and brothers in beating Samuel Birbeck.

HAD NO GUN.

The Chairman; Did you say you would blow their___ brains out? – Yes, sir.

Who were you addressing? – The whole crowd on the shore, who were threatening the Alexanders.

Had you anything to shoot them with? – No, sir.

Wm. Alexander, sen., replying to Mr. Poole, said he went down to the shore about half past eight. He was carrying a hazel walking stick owing to his leg being bad. He went in the direction of the nets, and there saw his sons, Sam and Jim. He shouted to his sons "come off" as they were quarrelling.

Mr. Poole; Where were the Birbecks; could you see them? – Yes, though it was a bit hazy.

Witness added that he saw the three Birbecks and his own sons running when Harry Birbeck left them and came straight on to him and struck him with the spade. His son, Samuel, was surrounded by Birbecks. He denied that he and his sons beat Samuel Birbeck that night, and he also said he had not seen the latter that night.

The four Alexanders were committed for trial at the next Lancaster Assizes , and allowed bail in the sum of £25. Mr. Poole also made an application for a certificate for legal aid, and this was granted.

A follow up article was reported after a hearing at the Lancaster Assizes by;

North-Western Daily Mail, 6th June 1931.

THE ASKAM SANDS AFFAIR. JUDGE'S STERN WARNING TO ACCUSED.

MISSING MAN'S POSITION.

The jury at Lancaster Assizes on Friday, returned a verdict of "not guilty" in the case in which William Alexander, junr., James Alexander, and Samuel Alexander, of Askam, were jointly charged with wounding Samuel Birbeck. With intent to do grievous bodily harm, on April 23rd.

William Alexander, sen., father of the three men, was also committed for trail, but in the meantime had disappeared .

Mr. Blackledge, who prosecuted, said that although the man's clothes had been found on the shore, his body had not been recovered. Therefore, he had to presume he was still alive, and he applied for a bench warrant.

Granting the application, Mr. Justice Macnaughten said it was not a new device either in fact or fiction for a person to leave his clothes on the shore in order that people might presume him dead.

Prosecuting, Mr. Blackledge said the Alexanders and Birbecks had fishery interests and also lusty families. The trouble seemed to have arisen over the struggle between the parties for the best places on the shore to put their nets. On the evening in question Samuel Birbeck, who was not interested in the fishing, went for a walk along the shore, and was suddenly set upon by the Alexanders, one of whom had a double barrelled gun, and the others carried stakes. He sustained injuries about the head and was also bruised extensively about the body. It was further alleged that he was thrown into the channel, which contained two feet of water, and then William Alexander, junr., when the crowd which had been attracted looked like interfering, threatened to blow out anyone's brains who dared to come near.

The defence set up by Mr. Rupert Greene for the accused was a complete denial that either of the accused men inflicted on Birbeck the injuries he sustained. Wm. Alexander, junr., alleged that he took a stake from him in self-defence, but the other prisoners denied having touched him.

The jury were absent only a few minutes before they returned a verdict of not guilty.

Discharging the accused, his Lordship advised them to go home. "Let there be no more fighting in Askam," he added.

Addressing the jury in relation to the case in which Henry Birbeck was alleged to have wounded two of the Alexanders with intent to do grievous bodily harm, the Judge said it might be that that the jury thought that there had been six of one and half a dozen of the other.

The Foreman; Yes, sir.

The Judge; If the Crown were to proceed with either indictment your verdict would probably be the same? – In all probability.

His Lordship (to Mr. Blackledge); Under those circumstances I think it would be right for the Crown to offer no evidence against Henry Birbeck.

After formal proceedings, Birbeck was found not guilty and discharged. His Lordship remarking that he hoped this sort of thing would not be repeated in Askam. If there was any further disturbance and either parties who had been there that day were concerned in it, it would go hard with them next time.

His Lordship directed that the warrant for the apprehension of the father should remain, as there was certain evidence against him which was admissible against the other prisoners in his absence which might have had an influence in the case already heard.

After this, the fighting had stopped between our families. William Alexander, senr., was never seen again in Askam, although, as you can imagine there was much speculation and rumour as to what became of him and I have come across three stories. Firstly, he committed suicide by drowning off Askam Pier. Secondly, the Birbeck's had killed him with a fork and dumped him in the sea. Thirdly, he had been seen at Preston train station waiting for a train to Liverpool. What I do know is that even in the 1950's the warrant for his arrest was still active as a new police constable came down the shore one day asking our family regarding his whereabouts and stated they were still looking for him!

On the 24th November 1931, William Birbeck went missing. He attended their net with his brother Henry. They did so as the tide was coming in and in thick fog. Henry made it back ashore near Roanhead, however William's body was found washed up on Angerton Marsh, near Foxfield on the 7th March 1932. The Birbeck family did very little fishing after this.

Manchester Courier and Lancashire General Advertiser, 2nd November 1850.

Some men quarrelled on Thursday week on the Duddon sands respecting the right to some flukes which had been cast over the bar. They came to blows, and Samuel Todd, who had a gun, shot John Kelly, a carpenter, through the heart.

Soulby's Ulverston Advertiser, 15th July 1880.

ULVERSTON POLICE COURT. FISHERY CASE.

William Bird was charged with illegally fishing for salmon in the Duddon, on the 11th.

Mr. Jackson prosecuted for the Fishery Conservators, and Mr. Pearson was for the defence. Mr. Jackson said that a little before 11 p.m. on Sunday night, defendant was found shooting his nets in a portion of the Duddon. When spoken to, he refused to draw out his nets, under the idea that if no fish were seen, no offence could be proved.

Michael Bird and John Procter, saw Bird and others shooting the nets. They could feel fish in the nets. William Bird said that if they saw no fish, they could make nothing of him. Michael Bird cut off a piece of the net as a witness.

Mr. Pearson said that on the day in question, defendant had taken out a pleasure party in his boat. In the evening he went to his large boat, where he slept, but before going to bed, he examined his nets in the smaller boat, as much mischief is frequently done amongst the fisherman's nets.

He found the net in a sad state, and twisted and twined all over the boat. Whilst he was straightening the net, Michael Bird and John Procter came up and, and cut his net, thinking, no doubt, he was fishing. They had long had spite against Wm. Bird.

Thomas Winder Harrison was with Wm. Bird at the time, and gave corroborative evidence.

By Mr. Jackson; The whole of the net was put in the hole; I held one part; There was another young man there, and he helped to put the net in. – Defendant was fined £5 and costs.

| seven |

OTHER BITS AND BOBS

Here is a sea fisheries report published in 1879, into the state of the fishing industry throughout England and Wales. An inquiry was held at Furness Abbey Hotel, where Millom and Furness fishermen attended and gave their account, below are the testimonies relating to the Duddon Estuary.

REPORT BY
FRANK BUCKLAND, Esq.,
And
SPENCER WALPOLE, Esq.,
INSPECTORS OF FISHERIES FOR ENGLAND AND WALES
AND COMMISSIONERS FOR SEA FISHERIES ON THE SEA FISHERIES OF ENGLAND AND WALES.
PRESENTED TO BOTH HOUSES OF PARLIAMENT BY COMMAND OF HER MAJESTY

FURNESS ABBEY HOTEL, FURNESS, THURSDAY, 9TH MAY, 1878.
PRESENT; Frank Buckland and Spencer Walpole, Esquires.

Sir James Ramsden, ex-mayor of Barrow in Furness and a Director of the Furness Railway. – The total quantity of cockles sent away by (Furness) railway in 1877 was 2,254 tons. Believes this is not more than are usually sent away.
"Askam – 220 tons."
"Dalton – 80 tons."
"Millom – 343 tons."

William Slater, farmer, of Cark (*Park farm, Nr Askam*). – Has seen many mussels here. The largest bed he ever saw was near Roanhead, on the east side of the Duddon Estuary. This was a large bed covering several acres. They are now gone entirely. They were destroyed by being used for manure. The destruction was by human agency. They have may have been partly sanded up, but believes they were destroyed by over-fishing. The largest were sold in the market; the little ones were used as manure, and scores of tons were wasted altogether. The fishery has entirely disappeared. They were chiefly destroyed in one year. This was about 30 years ago. There are mussels further out in deeper water. It would be desirable to restore this bed of mussels, and the farmers would not now take them away. The fishermen here use lug-worms and not mussels for bait. This mussel bed is claimed by the Duke of Buccleuch, the fishery by the Duke of Devonshire.

Cockles in the Duddon Estuary are ten times as important as mussels ever were. Forty years ago the cockle trade in Duddon was three or four times as great as it is now. Thinks the cockles were destroyed by over-fishing. There were regiments of women continually employed in cockling. This last winter has been exceptionally good, but before the last winter the trade had much fallen off. The cockles are never good in the months without the r's. Cannot say whether it would be desirable to have a close season. The cocklers used to tread the cockles out of the sand by stamping with their feet. The small cockles were left to be killed by gulls, and the large ones only were taken away.

Thinks the black-headed gulls and other gulls are destructive to the cockles. The gulls eat all carrion. Cannot say that the gulls have increased since the Sea Birds Act. Thinks that they have decreased. It is the small black-headed gull that follows the plough.

The fluke fishery is nothing like it used to be. It has fallen off 19 parts out of 20 or more. Cartful's of flukes used to be taken away. Is speaking of the fluke fishery in Duddon Estuary. There is little trawling in Duddon. The shrimping in Duddon is not one twentieth part of the shrimping in Morecambe Bay.

The flukes in Duddon are white flukes. They cannot be caught in a trawl. The failure began more than 30 years ago. Cannot say what these flukes live on.

Formerly there was no trawling outside. There is now a large fleet of trawlers outside of Walney Island. Has seen cockles and mussels inside the flukes. The failure in the mussels preceded the failure in flukes. It is reasonable to think that the falling off of the mussels and cockles may be connected with the falling off of the flukes.

John Bird, fisherman, of Duddon. – Is 74 years old. When he began fishing there were 10 times as many flukes as there are now. Used to catch them with fixed nets, rising and falling with the tide. When he began fishing there were no trawl boats outside; there are now above 100. They come from Fleetwood and Liverpool. Believes that in frosty weather the white flukes go off into deep water, and are caught by the trawlers. In frosty weather they always go off into deep water, "neck over heels," and in fine weather they come back again. The flukes began decreasing about 10 years ago. The fluke fishers catch little cockles and little mussels, the size of Indian corn.

There are not so many cockles or mussels as there were 10 years ago. The seagulls and oyster catchers eat many hundred tons of cockles and mussels of the size of marbles. The shells may be found lying on the sand like hailstones. These birds have increased in great numbers. People are now not allowed to kill the gulls, and cannot drive them off. If he were allowed to shoot the gulls he would take a 10s. gun licence. The gulls eat the flukes out of the nets before he can get them; they eat many a basketful before he can get out to them. The oyster catchers (sea pies) are of no value to anyone. Believes if he had the liberty to kill the sea pies he would have as many flukes as ever. The gulls and sea pies are the ruin of the shell fisheries, and the loss of the shell fish is the cause of the failure of the flukes. Duddon is no river for shrimps, and there are very few shrimpers.

The cockles breed in May. The smallest cockle he ever saw was about the size of a pin's head. This was in June. There are male and female cockles with roe and milt. The cockle spawn does not float. The little cockles are found on the same ground as the old cockles, and little pinholes may be seen in the sand, made by these little cockles. The little cockles surround the big cockles. The cockles are increased by the ground being worked. The working turns the sand over. The cockle is barely an inch under the sand.

Does not know what the cockle eats.

The sea birds get a thousand cockles to the cockler's quart. If Duddon Sands had been free from birds Duddon Sands would be worth more than any estate in Furness. Has seen 180 people cockling in Furness, and now the birds get what these people used to pick. Sends his cockles to Blackburn, Manchester, Bolton and Keighley.

My lad Billy inspecting the Flukes in the stake net at Roanhead in 2018.
(Kevin Alexander collection).

William Bird, fisherman, Askam. – Has been an "inside" and "outside" fisher. Has trawled outside Walney Island. Catches plaice, cod, ray, &c, outside. Never catches white flukes outside of Walney Island. Never catches white flukes in the winter outside. There are both plaice and white flukes in the Duddon Estuary. Thinks the trawling outside has interfered with the estuary fishing.

The Furness men have been in the habit of riddling their catches. The Morecambe men do not riddle theirs. The Morecambe men have no time to riddle their shrimps. They riddle them at home when they are dead, and sell the small ones for manure. There ought to be a law compelling everyone to riddle his shrimps. This could be carried out if there were a man stationed at Morecambe to see to the riddling of the shrimps.

The chain-trawl catches more shrimps and flukes than the beam-trawl. The shrimps are on the sand.

John Graham, fisherman. – Lives at Holborn Hill, Millom. Fishes for salmon when he can get them. Has never fished for flukes, but sometimes takes them. There are not one hundredth part of the flat fish there used to be. Has large stake net for salmon,. Catches also mullet, bass, white flukes, plaice fluke, turbot and soles. Has fished the Duddon for 33 years. Thirty three years ago there was not a trawl in the Duddon. The trawling began 28 years ago. Within the last 8 or 10 years the flat fish have fallen off most bitterly, cannot say how many trawlers there are in the channel.

Is in favour of a close season for fluking. The plaice fluke is here in September. The spawn is in them in February and March. They spawn on the sea shore. The plaice fluke's spawn is blue, the white fluke's spawn is pink. The white flukes spawn in the river higher up. The trawlers trawl a good way up the river. Could not say how many trawlers there are in Duddon. Is in favour of a close season for cockles also, and indeed for everything. Cannot say whether there ought to be a close season for birds.

Henry Bell, of Millom. – Follows fluke fishing. Has been fishing for them for 70 years. There are not a tenth of the flukes there used to be. Thinks the flukes should have a four month's close season. February, March, April and May should be the close season. This would prevent little fish being destroyed at that time. Would stop shrimping also at that time. Cannot say why the flukes have fallen off. They have slackened terribly since the shrimpers came in. There were seven shrimpers last year.

Michael Bird, son of John Bird. – Is a shrimper in Duddon. Only three boats there. Catches flukes all through the winter, when flukes are in best condition. When he is shrimping sometimes catches many small fish.

Riddles the shrimps. If a close season were made from February to April he could not live. The close season would do no good. The cockles and mussels are choked by the channel silting.

My lad Doug with an example of brack beside Lots Channel.
(Kevin Alexander collection).

Soulby's Ulverston Advertiser and General Intelligencer, 18th October 1900.

ANOTHER BODY FOUND ON THE SANDS.

On Saturday afternoon, about three o'clock, as a man named Gillbanks, of Stafford Street, Askam, was walking on the Duddon Sands, near Sandscale, he came across a headless body of a man, which had been left by the tide. The hands and feet were also missing. There was no clothing on the body. P.S. Carr, of Askam, had the remains removed to a shed behind the Askam Hotel, on The Lots. This is the second body washed up on Duddon Sands within a month. The remains, which have not been identified, were duly interred in the Ireleth Churchyard on Tuesday afternoon.

Ulverston Mirror, 18th October 1879.

On Thursday last a large fishing frog, or sea devil, was caught on Duddon Sands by John Laybourne, fisherman. It measured upwards of four feet in length, and was exhibited for several days. *(Very likely to be type of Anglerfish from the deep seas, and an extremely rare find).*

Soulby's Ulverston Advertiser, 12th May 1870.

LARGE FISH.

On Friday last, four fishermen. Whilst out on the Duddon with their boat, noticed a large fish, which they attempted to capture. Having tied their knives to the oars, they attacked it, and a serious fight ensued. For a long time the issue was doubtful, the fish almost drowning the men with the water it spouted; it also seized the boat with its teeth, and tore away several planks. Ultimately, however, it was killed, and taken to Barrow, where it was purchased by Mr. Goddard, and had its intestines taken out, and the carcase cured. It measures 10ft. long, and weighed from seven to eight cwt. It is now being exhibited at the Piel Castle Inn, in this town.

Millom Gazette, 5th September 1905.

THE BOISTEROUS WEATHER.

HIGH TIDES AT HAVERIGG.

DAMAGE TO BOATS, etc.

ROADS SUBMURGED BY WATER.

On Tuesday evening last, a very severe gale passed over the district. Heavy showers, accompanied by a strong south-west wind, and dark heavy clouds, prevailed throughout. Spring tides were approaching, and it was quickly noted that if the wind kept on it would not be a matter for surprise if the Haverigg roads were submerged by high tides.

Several boatmen on Wednesday morning, seeing that the wind had, if anything, increased in its force, wisely decided to bring their boats up into a place of safety.

Heavy showers of sand, were encountered, and the sea was very high. This wind kept and the boatmen had as much as they could do to remove their boats.

The tide rose with alarming rapidity, and at eleven o'clock the children were released from school in order that they may might reach their homes before the tide prevented them.

A large number of people made their way to the sea shore. Here a stormy but interesting spectacle met their view. High and large waves were rushing in, while between the two ends of the new wall, the water rushed in with great speed.

As the water advanced it was predicted that some of the boats would be very fortunate if they weathered the gale. Several boats had already sunk, one belonging to Mr. Bird, and another belonging to Mr. Anthony Myers were the first pair to go down.

A yacht, owned by Mr. Edward Metters, was the next victim claimed. The yacht in the first place listed towards the sea. The tide was running in a wild manner. A wave or two knocked the yacht in an upright position, and receded, another sent the unfortunate boat on its other side, and from now till it foundered it rode very heavy.

Another boat owned by Mr. J. Thomas, was next claimed by the sea, it taking very few of the many tremendous waves to sink it. Grave fears were entertained for the boats that had been so unfortunately swamped, the possibility of their breaking their moorings or bumping, themselves to pieces on the bottom being realised as the greatest danger. At noon the tide had broken over the road along Pool Side, and Sea View. Traffic was completely blocked, and most of the houses were entered. The Harbour Hotel was inundated, and the water also found the way up Bank Field Road, and at the back of Sea View.

A large quantity of sand, stones etc., were scattered all over the road. The waves broke over the slatings in front of Concrete Square, and water of a considerable depth completely surrounded the houses. Here again many people gathered to watch the scene.

Many anxious looks were cast towards the boats left standing. These, however, rode out in safety, and escaped scatheless. Tide boards were seen here and there, while at the Harbour Hotel corner the groups of onlookers were being photographed as they stood, with the tide near them by Mr. Doughty.

Altogether the scene was a novel one, the water broke into Concrete Square gardens, as well as several fields along the river side.

At the turn of the tide the wind gradually calmed down. The fury of the sea was abated, and after this there was not much fear of the tide doing any more damage. All that remained now was to learn the fate of the foundered ones.

WILD SCENE IN DUDDON ESTUARY.

RAILWAY UNDER WATER.

TRAINS FLOODED.

During Wednesday morning the full force of the gale was felt in the Duddon Estuary. With the rising tide a heavy sea began to run and with high wind that was blowing long before the tide was at its full a large tract of land was flooded on both the Lancashire and Cumberland side of the river. At Green Road the Black Beck overflowed its banks and a huge lake was formed, stretching from the railway bridge well on to Lady Hall. At Foxfield the water beat with considerable force outside the station. Such was the height and force of the water that a row boat was washed into the road leading from the station to Park's Farm, the latter being three parts surrounded by water.

At Kirkby the floods were very heavy. The water had risen over the waterline of the Furness Railway, and as the 10.54 train from Barrow passed the waves were dashing against the wheels of the engine and coaches, some of the carriages being flooded. Some sheep had a very narrow escape near Kirkby. They were swimming for a long time until they were rescued.

The scene in the estuary was a wild one. The high wind caught up the waves with great force dashing the spray for considerable distances. The huge rock Dunnerholm was one mass of spray. Just after noon the wind subsided, and the tide going-out, the estuary was comparatively calm again.

Millom Gazette, 16th May 1902.

CURIOUS CATCH BY HAVERIGG FISHERMAN.

On Tuesday evening last, as Mr. S. Sage and Co. were out fishing, they caught a very hideous, and ugly-looking fish. For a long time the name of this fish could not be ascertained.

On looking up a fishery book entitled "The Sea and its Wonders," it was discovered that it was a cuttle-fish, one of the kinds which is called a poulpe. A full-sized one is a very dangerous fish, and has been known to kill everything that comes before it. This fish can now be seen at Mrs. Sage's, Sea View, Haverigg.

Millom Gazette, 11th August 1922.

HAVERIGG REGATTA.

The racing events in connection with the above regatta took place on Monday and Tuesday last in what has now come to be known (as far as Monday was concerned) as true Haverigg regatta weather.

With the exception of the rain, however, the conditions for good racing could not have been improved upon, a fresh breeze from N.E. with a smooth sea making for fast sailing. Class B for decked boats over 30 feet brought out three starters, viz.: Eleanor (Millom), Maud (Haverigg), and Ploughboy (Barrow).

The start was timed at 11.38.13, Eleanor and Maud getting away well together, leaving Ploughboy struggling with a recalcitrant topsail, which practically put her out of the race from the beginning. The course was from Haverigg round no. 1 buoy, back to Haverigg, round no. 6 out to no. 5, back over the same course round no. 6, and finish at Haverigg. The race developed into a duel between Eleanor and Maud. At the end of the first round the boats were timed : Eleanor 12.24.50, Maud 12.27.32.

L to R, J.Walters, W.Davis, Edgar Jeffery and W.Mellon. Haverigg men with a trophy and prize, likely from a Sailing Regatta.
(Courtesy of John Jeffery and family of Haverigg).

The second round was practically a repetition of the first, with Eleanor increasing her lead all the time from Maud, whether in running free or beating. Ploughboy hung on in a sporting manner all round the course, but her initial handicap was too great to be made up, and in any case she would not of saved her time from either Eleanor or Maud on the day's sailing. A fast and well sailed race ended: Eleanor 1.7.37, Maud 1.11.19, Ploughboy 1.19.43.

Classes E. and F., the former for half-decked boats over 20 feet and the latter for open boats up to 20 feet, were started together at 11.35, the starters in Class E being: Bertha (Millom), Marian (Millom), Polly (Haverigg), and Gundreda (Barrow). Those in Class F were: Thistle (Haverigg), Edith (Haverigg), Agnes (Barrow), Pearl (Haverigg), Clara (Haverigg), Audrey (Haverigg), Ida (Haverigg), Merrymaid (Haverigg).

Dealing with the four boats in Class E first, all with the exception of Marion got away well, and after fetching out to no. 10 and returning to Haverigg there was little to choose between the boats. The leaders were timed at the end of the first round: Bertha 12.27.55, Polly 12.30.28, Marian having retired soon on with a broken gaff jaw. Bertha and Polly sailed a neck-and-neck race all round the course, with Bertha just leading. The latter lost ground on the final beat back to the line, and a most exciting finish to a hard sailed race was timed: Bertha 1.29.35, Polly 1.29.37, Gundreda 1.41.1.

TUESDAY.

The weather on this day was all against good racing, there being only a very light breeze from the west, which practically turned the races into drifting matches. The races for Classes C, D, and G were down for decision. Class C starters were: Mary Ellen (Haverigg) and Sunbeam (Haverigg). Class D: Nancy (Barrow), Jaunita (Barrow), Eileen (Barrow) and Gundreda (Barrow). Class G: Mussel King (Millom), Ginger (Haverigg), Bertha (Haverigg).

All classes were started together at 12.7.45. Owing to lack of wind, the courses were kept as short as possible, viz.: for C and D classes, from Haverigg out to no. 10 buoy, back to Haverigg round no. 6 buoy, and finish at Haverigg. That for Class G was from Haverigg out to no. 10 buoy and back to Haverigg. A fair start was made, and mainly through the effect of the tide the boats worked down to no. 10, after which the ebb brought them back, what little wind there was being just sufficient to keep the larger boats on the coarse. The smaller boats were carried well outside the line, having to work back to the finish. Nancy and Mary Ellen had worked out a lead in their classes, but this was neutralized on rounding no. 6 buoy, when all boats were bunched together, endeavouring to stem the strong ebb with what little wind there was. About 2.15.0 the wind freshened, which enabled a very un-interesting race to be finished. Results:- Class C.- Mary Ellen 3.19.28, Sunbeam 3.26.10.

Class D.- Gundreda 3.19.33, Nancy, 3.22.20, Juanita 3.27.21. Eileen did not finish.

Class G:- Ginger 3.46.22, Mussel King and Bertha were not timed.

CHAS. C. COADE.

SPORTS.

The various sports attracted considerable interest, and resulted as follows:- Pony race.- 1st, A Gendle's Paddy (Millom); 2nd, Carpenter's What Ho (Haverigg); 3rd, Geo. Park's Hello (Haverigg). L. Park's Poverty came past the winng post before the others, but was disqualified for not going around the course, taking the wrong turn at one of the flag posts.

Girls' Race.-1st, M. Gibson (Millom); 2nd, M. Davidson (Millom); 3rd, B. Pattinson (Millom).

Boys' Race.- 1st, A. Sharp (Haverigg); 2nd, W. Coulson (Millom); 3rd, W. Harvey (Millom).

Ladies' Race.- 1st, Mrs. Vicars (Haverigg); 2nd, Miss Haslett (Millom); 3rd, Miss. Pennington (Millom).

Swimming (Adults).- 1st, W. Blackwell (Haverigg); 2nd, R .Jackson (Haverigg).

Sculling Race.- 1st, D. Milton (Haverigg); 2nd, Ronald Singleton (Haverigg).

Walking the Greasy Bowsprit.- No competitor succeeded in reaching the end, and the first prize was divided between Mr. Foster (a visitor) and Mr. MacMeekin (Millom), the third prize being awarded to Mr. Macahodle.

Swimming (youths).- 1st, W. Fleming (Haverigg); 2nd, Wm. Clemens (Haverigg); 3rd, R. Fleming. (Haverigg).

Dancing was held in connection with the Regatta in the Bankfield Road Schools on Monday and Tuesday evenings, a whist drive also being conducted on the Monday.

It was noted on Tuesday that a motor boat from Barrow, capable of accommodating about twenty passengers, was plying for hire from the beach, and apparently doing good business. What has become of the enterprise so commonly associated with Haverigg people?

The earliest Haverigg Regatta that I've come across was held in 1864 and became an annual event but for one reason or another, it would stop for a time then be revived and then stop again. It turns out the Regatta was revived a total of three times and had completely stopped by 1930.

Millom Gazette, 15th September 1922.

Though the Millom Regatta started in a small way, there can be no doubt as to its great success. Never before at any time have so many people been seen on Crab Marsh, not even when one or other of the Millom-built vessels were launched.

From an atmospherical point of view the day was all that could be desired, and competitors and spectators alike experienced an enjoyable afternoon. In the boat racing competitions few except those who were experts could find any excitement in the manoeuvring of the different vessels. Still, it was this aquatic competition that attracted such a big crowd.

The smooth waters of the Duddon Estuary are, if not in every other respect, at least from a spectators point of view, very well adapted for such events, and there is every prospect of future regattas being even more successful than the one held on Saturday last. Everything passed off most successfully, and the public were thoroughly satisfied with the whole proceedings.

A photograph showing the Mary Ellen of Haverigg.
(Courtesy of John Jeffery and family of Haverigg).

The shimmering waters presented a pretty spectacle, and there was just sufficient wind to fill the sails of the competing boats. But whilst everything passed off so pleasantly on Saturday, circumstances have not always been so happy at that particular place, and the sands have been the scene of several tragedies in the past. Prior to the construction of the railway the most frequented route to get from Millom to Kirkby or other parts of Furness was over the sands. From Millom the road commenced at the end of the present Lancashire road, and, skirting in a direction of Green Road, the Duddon was forded almost opposite Kirkby.

The incoming and outgoing tides, however, left somewhat dangerous holes which some times were covered with sand and formed a kind of quagmire or quicksand, and the worst of these had to be carefully avoided by man and beast. Guides were kept in Millom whose duty it was to test the sands and show the safe road to the other side. Brogs – long poles to which brushwood was attached, were fixed in the sands to indicate to pedestrians and drivers of vehicles the best route to take in order to safely negotiate the somewhat risky passage.

These brogs were the cause of a very amusing incident somewhere over 100 years ago. It was the time when Napoleon threatened to invade England, and the farmers and townsfolk were up in arms, determined to do or die should the French carry out their threat.

At this time there were rumours that a French expedition was likely to land somewhere on the Cumberland coast. The news was brought to Broughton, and most of the residents were in fear and trepidations. A sea fog spreading over the sands, some mischievous fellow originated the idea that the enemy had utilised the fog for concealment, and were making their way up the Duddon in flat-bottomed boats. A few of more venturesome spirits went down by Greety Gate to Foxfield to ascertain if anything could be discovered.

The fog at the time had enveloped the whole Estuary, and was rolling inland, but, as sometimes happens, it was close to the ground, allowing objects to be pretty clearly seen above it. The sands were well covered with brogs, and the tops of them could be distinctly seen above the mist. The exploring party from Broughton imagined these to be the masts of vessels carrying the French expeditionary forces, and at once hurried back to Broughton with the information that the French were upon them, and that several vessels were sailing up the Duddon. It was only a matter of a few minutes before the whole population of the village were making for the hills as fast as they could travel. It was late in the evening when the exodus commenced, so that men, women, and children had to spend the night in the open – with one exception, however.

One Dixon, noted for the quantity of beer he could consume, made his way to the Old King's Head, and as nothing was protected, he sampled one barrel of beer after the another, forgetting to turn of the taps, and the whole contents of the barrels were thus wasted. One half-witted lad, under the impression that he would be cut to pieces, made his way to Ulpha to some secluded place among the hills, and was discovered some days afterwards in a half-starved condition. From a point of vantage one of the benighted residents in the morning took observations, and, seeing nothing unusual, drew nearer, and found, instead of being occupied by French soldiers, that the whole place was deserted. Word was sent round, and people flocked back to their homes. For some time the youths who raised the alarm had a bad time, and residents at Coniston, Millom and Kirkby for many a long day had a good laugh over the "Battle of Broughton."

An original Ordnance Survey map published in 1914 showing the channels positions at that time.
(Kevin Alexander collection).

ACKNOWLEDGEMENTS

As this is my first ever publication I have found it to be a daunting experience, however the subject being that of the Duddon Sands has made it worth while to me, and I am forever grateful for all the help I have received in this endeavour along the way.

Thanks go to Cumbria Archive and Local Studies Centre, Barrow for all of their help and support and kind permission to use photographs and material they hold.

Thanks also to the family of John Jeffery of Haverigg for kindly allowing me the use of photographs. Thanks to Norman Pascoe for the use of his Dunnerholme photograph. Thanks to Margaret Edmondson for the use of her photograph of Bird's Cottage, Roanhead.

Many thanks to my relatives and friends that have given me my knowledge of the Duddon, Walter Jinks, John Jinks and Muriel and Dennis Wilson you have been invaluable.

And thanks to Rachel Bloom and Mary Borgia for proofreading my mess.

Thanks to James Collinge and Dave Keenan for their assistance in getting to print.

And finally a sincere thank you to my wife Kelly and lads Doug and Bill, for their patience and understanding while I took many hours away engaged in compiling this work, and again to Kelly for being my final proof reader at the very end.

www.ingramcontent.com/pod-product-compliance
Lightning Source LLC
Chambersburg PA
CBHW060426010526
44118CB00017B/2382